Emotions
of Railway Art

Emotions

of Railway Art

101 new paintings from

The Guild of Railway Artists

Guild of Railway Artists website – www.railart.co.uk

First published in August 2011

A catalogue record for this book is available from the British Library

ISBN 978 1 84425 992 2

Library of Congress catalog card no 2011923595

Published by Haynes Publishing,
Sparkford, Yeovil, Somerset BA22 7JJ, UK
Tel: 01963 442030 Fax: 01963 440001
Int. tel: +44 1963 442030 Int. fax: +44 1963 440001
E-mail: sales@haynes.co.uk
Website: www.haynes.co.uk

Haynes North America Inc.,
861 Lawrence Drive, Newbury Park, California 91320, USA

Designed and typeset by Alan Gooch
Printed and bound in Italy by Rotolito Lombarda S.p.A.

ACKNOWLEDGEMENTS

The Guild of Railway Artists thanks the participating member artists for their support in this project and all members, both past and present, for their support for the Guild. Thanks are also given to the owners of certain depictions within this book for allowing their reproduction.

The Guild and Frank Hodges also thank, most sincerely, Mark Hughes, Peter Nicholson, Flora Myer and the staff of Haynes Publishing for their help, assistance and professionalism in bringing this book into being.

CONTENTS

FOREWORD

THE EXPLANATION OF our railway heritage to the broader public comes in many forms. Not surprisingly, we traditionally associate locomotives and rolling stock as being the principal means of putting across the message we want to convey. These can be truly dramatic and in the case of *Mallard* the initial WOW factor, and the look of awe and surprise on the faces of our visitors, is something to behold.

In addition, we of course make good use of our collections more broadly, and in many cases the smaller items in the National Collection can tell the story far more impressively and intelligently than perhaps a full size locomotive. But, no matter how we choose to present the railway story, the greatest challenge we face is that of setting the story in context. It is very difficult to convey in the modern age the full sense of what the railway used to be like. The National Railway Museum does it well but perhaps not quite well enough, although plans for the future will seek to ensure that the visitors don't just view a large collection of railway stock but also understand the story that it represents.

The vast array of preserved railways in this country also do a great job in setting in context the railway and its tradition. However, they too are subject to certain limitations and, although the atmosphere that, say, a high-speed mail drop at the Great Central Railway achieves is as close to the real thing as possible, we of course know that the full sense of sight, sound and smell will never be quite the same.

A painting, by contrast, is able to provide significant context. The NRM has an amazing collection of artwork. In most respects, that artwork record is almost exactly like the railway as it then was. We recognise the value of that collection and are in the closing stages of developing a dedicated art gallery.

Of course the artist is in a position not just to record the railway as it happened but also to undertake significant detailed research in order to genuinely recreate the full contextual experience that museums and preserved railway museums struggle to provide.

It is with that bold statement in mind that I welcome this opportunity to provide the foreword to *Emotions of Railway Art*. There can be no doubt that the collection of modern and contemporary railway painters and artists are providing that context through some quite glorious and factually created images. It therefore gives me the greatest pleasure both to officially recognise for the first time in my new role as Director of the NRM the work the Guild of Railway Artists does, and to state quite clearly that it has an important role to play in helping us to present and interpret the railway story.

Steve Davies MBE
Director, National Railway Museum

INTRODUCTION

FROM THE DAWN OF THE railway age the artist has been in the forefront of introducing illustrations of the many facets of railway to the public. The early artists found a new and exciting subject to depict with the introduction of the 'newfangled machine'. Some portrayed their scenes in a technically illustrative way, a record of a moment in time, much like a photograph (which still awaited its invention), with J.C. Bourne being perhaps one of the best known. Other artists took a different approach. They looked at the imagery of the railway, its moods, its settings, its sheer power, for their depictions. We still marvel today at the drawings and paintings J.C. Bourne and those of J.M.W. Turner, Claude Monet, Pierre Auguste Renoir, and Camille Pissaro in the new 'impressionist' style of their day, in which their 'emotions' for the subject are clearly seen within their works.

The artist, in whichever way they portray a scene, can lift it from the technically visual view of the eye and camera to a level and realm beyond, enticing the viewer to read the work much like a book. It is said that every picture tells a story – and there are many stories 'to read' in this book.

'Emotions' are the driving force when an artist puts brush to canvas or to paper. A scene is to be built up from a blank canvas to a completed painting. As well as the technical knowledge of the subject and the artistic technical skills required, it is that added 'emotion' that makes the picture come to life. However, in many cases though, it is not just the artist's emotions, but it is also those of the person who has commissioned the painting as well, that form a large part of the scene being depicted. Many of the members of the Guild of Railway Artists (GRA) accept commission work. It is their chosen career to paint or draw, and their income for their daily requirements has to be met from such work. The commissioner invariably has in mind, when placing work with an artist, what he or she expects in the finished product, and the artist has to include most, if not all, of the elements required by that person.

When asked by the publisher to produce a book, the Guild Council, after much discussion, came up with the theme 'Emotions'. The brief to the members of the GRA was as follows:

'We are looking for your personal emotions and memories etc. We are seeking pictures with heart and soul, pictures appealing to those who appreciate art as well as the railway element in its many facets. Let's really entertain the buyers of the book with a cornucopia of the best work ever seen. What scenes or subjects give you, the artist, that special tingle? – those are the ones to paint.'

In effect, we were asking our member artists to become their own 'commissioner', and to paint or draw the pictures, scenes or subjects they have always wanted to depict, but lack of time has not allowed them to do so.

Frank Hodges
Chief Executive Officer,
The Guild of Railway Artists

A HISTORY OF THE GUILD OF RAILWAY ARTISTS

THE GUILD OF RAILWAY ARTISTS has now been in existence for some 30 years. It has held exhibitions of members' work at venues throughout the country with, latterly, its main 'Annual' exhibition being staged at either Locomotion, The National Railway Museum at Shildon or the Kidderminster Railway Museum on the Severn Valley Railway.

The embryonic point of the Guild was the exhibition staged in 1977 by the Wight Locomotive Society, Midlands Area Group – a supporter group of the Isle of Wight Steam Railway, and the World Wildlife Fund – entitled 'Railart '77'. At that time, I was a member of the group staging the exhibition and little did I know what the future was going to bring.

It all started with an invitation to the president of the Wight Locomotive Society (WLS) to give a lecture at a group meeting in Leamington Spa – the president being none other than the well-known artist and wild life conservationist, David Shepherd. David suggested to our secretary, Andrew Britton, that he would let us have a couple of his paintings to display in a shop window in Leamington Spa to advertise the meeting. Things snowballed a little, and we found that we had the makings of an exhibition.

Following some press publicity a local and well-respected firm of auctioneers in the town, Messrs Locke and England, offered the use of their sale show room on the main street, free of charge, for our use for three weeks. We now had a venue, we also had more artists asking to take part – 'Railart '77' was on.

The exhibition, we believe, was the first ever staged specifically of railway art. The title 'Railart' was coined by Steve Johnson – who was very instrumental with me, in the subsequent formation of the Guild.

We thought we had found and contacted all the artists in Britain who painted railways – how wrong we were! Those we had tracked down

and who exhibited at the exhibition included David Shepherd, Sean Bolan, Hamilton Ellis, Lawrie Hammonds, George Heiron, Jim Petrie, Dick Potts, Victor Welch, Stella Whatley, and David Weston – and others, totalling some 20 artists. A total of 150 works of art were displayed by the artists – and, I hasten to say, 'unselected'! A souvenir brochure was produced, giving biographical details of the participants as well as a foreword by His Royal Highness, The Duke of Edinburgh.

For insurance purposes, the WLS had to mount overnight guard duties in the gallery. I did not have much to do with art at that time, but having the opportunity to live with the works on display certainly kindled an interest. The exhibition proved very successful as a one-off event, publicising the Isle of Wight Steam Railway, and supporting the World Wildlife Fund.

However, when Steve and I were transporting pictures back to artists and purchasers, which was a two-day trip with a box van from Leamington Spa to the South West – all along the south coast and into London before returning to Leamington – we discussed the idea of trying to keep the artists together. We spoke to a number of them on our travels, about our ideas, including David Shepherd (who put us up for the night). The comments received were largely in favour of our ideas to form some sort of association for railway artists.

The formation

After the exhibition, we went on with our normal lives and it was around six months afterwards that Captain Peter Manisty of the Association of Railway Preservation Societies contacted Steve, asking if he could advise him of artists' addresses in connection with the setting up of a memorial to John Scholes, the curator of the Museum of British Transport at

Clapham. This rekindled that idea of forming an association of railway artists. Steve and I contacted all the participating artists in 'Railart '77', together with a few others we had become aware of, suggesting the formation of such a body. This produced 14 artists who replied, agreeing to establish such an organisation. Those artists were asked for a small subscription to get the association going, and they became the 'Founder Members' of the Guild.

There were in fact 17 artists who signed up as the first members, these being: Don Breckon, Reginald Chamberlain, Terence Cuneo, Alan Fearnley, Maurice Gardner, Ken Glen, Lawrie Hammonds, Phil Hawkins, Mick Mabbutt, John Mason, Jim Petrie, Dick Potts, David Shepherd, Sam Wells, Stella Whatley, Arthur Wilkinson, and Rob Wilton.

The news of the formation of the group, now known as the Guild of Railway Artists, soon got around, mainly through the contacts of those founder members and editorials in the railway press. Further applications to join the throng soon started to pile into me, as by then, Steve and I were working as an ad-hoc administration team to get the Guild set up.

Although we thought we had found all the artists depicting railway in the country when we staged 'Railart '77', the membership doubled very quickly, and soon trebled from the initial founder members. Steve and I beavered away, gaining more supporters, trying to work out a draft constitution and producing the first newsletters, when our next landmark loomed.

A letter from a Miss Dawn Smith was received. She was organising the York International Railway Festival to be held in the city in late 1979. It was to be a four-day event and she stated that she had heard that we put on railway art exhibitions and asked if we could organise one for her for the York Festival. Our answer to her was, of course, yes. Our exhibition, the first ever by the Guild, was staged in October 1979, appropriately under the title 'Railart '79', at no lesser venue than the Guildhall in York, with some 157 pictures on display from 37 artists, supplemented with a display of railway heraldic coats of arms by collector Gerald Hartley.

At the close of the exhibition we held the first general meeting of the Guild and again, the venue appropriately, was the Guildhall. (I still think of York's Guildhall as our Guild hall!)

Steve and I took the top table and introduced ourselves to the assembled artists, to start the meeting. First on the agenda was the election of a chairman. We had spotted a very smart gentleman in the audience who seemed to fit the bill – and as no nominations had been received prior to the meeting, we asked Alan Fearnley whether he would consider taking the chairmanship. I think that even before he could answer, the members present had decided, with a forest of hands being displayed for an affirmative 'Yes'. Alan was promptly elevated to the top table.

We had placed before the members a draft constitution to be discussed and hopefully accepted by the meeting. Steve and I (perhaps rather foolishly), suggested to the assembly, that we were willing to carry on as the administration team, with Steve as co-ordinator and myself as secretary, until elections took place to form a proper management committee with the appropriate officers, for a period of no more than two years. Little did I know at that time that the two years was going to extend to 30 years plus!

The Guild was on its way and the next exhibition soon loomed upon us, by invitation of the organisers of the Great Railway Exposition to be held at Liverpool Road Station, Manchester during August and September 1980. Again, the title 'Railart' was used, this time 'Railart '80'. The exhibition was mounted in the waiting room of the historic station – the country's first 'Inter-City' station, and now part of the Museum of Science and Industry. Due to space constraints the numbers of submissions were down quite considerably as we only allowed a maximum of two pictures per artist. However, we were able to put on a display of 46 works from 26 members.

The first 'Full Members' of the Guild were elected: Paul Gribble, Alan Fearnley, Lawrie Hammonds, Jim Petrie, and Stella Whatley – followed quite quickly with further Full Members including Phil Hawkins, John Wigston, Peter Annable, etc. through adjudication panel meetings.

Two artists were elected as the first 'Fellows' of the Guild at the 1982 annual general meeting, these being Terence Cuneo and David Shepherd. The Fellowship is the highest accolade the Guild pays to an artist. Only three further artists have since received this accolade: Philip D. Hawkins in 1998, John Austin in 2006, and Malcolm Root in 2010. At that same meeting, Sir William McAlpine (the Hon William McAlpine, as he was then) was asked to become our President, a post that he graciously accepted and today is now our Patron.

Over the next two years we staged exhibitions in Sunderland, Crystal Palace (an international railway exhibition staged by Dawn Smith), and a show in my own home town of Warwick, in the Warwickshire Museum.

It was interesting to see that when ploughing through the files while putting this potted history of the Guild together, it was noted that at the 1982 AGM the thorny question of selection arose, with that being, in effect, a show of hands by five or so Full Members. It was however agreed at the end of the day, that the Guild should continue with the system as operating at that time.

Over the years method has been enhanced, and it is now carried out by an electronic voting system consisting of two-way switches which are linked to a diode display giving the results of the votes (green for yes, red for no), which the panel members cannot see. It is normal practice for the panel to consist of nine Full Members, however by invitation of the chairman of the panel, Associate Members may also sit-in on a selection panel. I think the selection process has probably had more airtime than any other subject appertaining to the Guild and I know it is probably the most difficult task we give our members. The subject of art is a very subjective one!

In 1982, we were invited to stage our first exhibition at the National Railway Museum, York in what was the North Gallery, which proved a very successful exhibition with 83 works on display, including some Cuneo's. Since that exhibition, the Guild has had very good links with the museum over the years, with five further exhibitions being staged at the NRM itself and another three at its outstation, 'Locomotion' at Shildon.

By that year, we had sorted out the Aims and the Constitution and at the annual general meeting a 'management advisory committee' was elected. The members who offered their services for this were Sean Bolan, Norman Elford, Alan Fearnley, Paul Gribble, Philip Hawkins, Mick Mabbutt, C. Stephenson-Mole, and Barry Walding.

Well, Steve and I thought now they had a committee, for the second time it was the opportunity to exit. Not so. Steve was elected as honorary co-ordinator and I was elected as honorary administrator to carry out the day-to-day running of the Guild. By this time the Guild had just topped the 100 mark in its membership.

Our next milepost was the 150th anniversary of the forming of the Great Western Railway, being celebrated in 1985. Steve had some ideas. He suggested to the committee that we produce a book of members' work, and hire an exhibition train from BR to travel around the country promoting it. Yes, Steve was an ideas man!

We contacted publisher Colin Judge (then of Oxford Publishing Co.) about our ideas for a book commemorating the GWR's anniversary. Colin, at that time, was just in the throes of selling the OPC imprint to Blandford Press. However, we had a meeting with him and the new owner of OPC, Richard Erven, in Warwick to discuss the ideas. We just had the idea – no works to show them, no text – just our thoughts on the matter. Straight away, Richard fell in love with the concept and told us to go ahead – he would publish it. Our first major project was now underway and it proved a resounding success for the Guild. *The Great Western Collection* was published under the Blandford Press imprint with a large quantity being provided to the Railway Book Club under its own, appropriately titled Guild Publishing imprint.

In total, some 28,500 copies of the original version of the book were produced, with another 6,000 printed five years later by New Orchard Editions.

As to the exhibition of the works contained in the book, the original idea of having our own train proved too expensive. However, we were asked to be part of British Rail's own GWR150 exhibition train touring the country during 1985. We took up the offer, even though we were aware it was going to cost around £10,000. We visited some 40 locations within England and we were then invited by the organisers of the 3rd International Model Railway Festival, being held in the Messe Frankfurt, to stage the exhibition there, with full expenses being paid – an offer we could not refuse.

The Guild was now at long last becoming recognised and it proved a very busy year, especially as Steve or I alternately needed to visit the exhibition train each week to service the display – including cleaning the marks on the glass covering the Cuneo paintings so that the' mouse' could be seen.

Following *The Great Western Collection* our next book was entitled *To the Seaside*, an evocative selection of paintings recalling those journeys most of us will remember from our early days. It included an introduction to the subject written by then *Daily Telegraph* columnist and BBC Radio 2 Jazz Presenter, the late Peter Clayton and was published by David and Charles in 1990. The book was reprinted as a softback in 2005 under the title *Great Railway Paintings Inspired by the Seaside*.

Our next book was in celebration of the 100th anniversary of *The Railway Magazine*. Entitled *A Century of Railway Art* it was published in 1996 by Oxford Publishing Co., owned at that time by Haynes Publishing, the publisher of this current book. Words were by Peter W.B. Semmens, the former Deputy Head of the National Railway Museum and the magazine's Chief Correspondent, and a foreword was contributed by His Royal Highness The Duke of Gloucester.

Our last book, *Along Artistic Lines*, a celebration of two centuries of railways in Britain, was published in 2003 by Atlantic Publishers in conjunction with the National Railway Museum. An introduction to the subject was provided by Beverley Cole, who at that time was the Curator of the National Railway Museum's Pictorial Collection.

Since formation, the GRA has staged over 70 exhibitions and hung over 4,000 works of art.

The Committee, Guild Council, Chairmen and Presidents

The GRA Committee, now called the Guild Council, has seen many changes of membership over the years. However, we do have some stalwarts still with us from the first elected committees – Phil Hawkins elected in 1982, and Ellis James-Robertson in 1983. I think both should receive long-service awards!

We have also had a few changes of chairmen, now presidents. Alan Fearnley continued in post until 1984, with Sean Bolan taking over the seat from that year until 1988 when he was replaced by Philip D. Hawkins. Phil served as our chairman until 1995. I seem to remember he did, on a number of occasions, ask if anyone else would like the job, but without success. However, in 1995 after a change in our constitution, when it was decided to move Sir William McAlpine to being a Patron of the Guild (as well as electing Pete Waterman as a further Patron), the post of Chairman was re-titled President.

Phil continued in this role until 1998 when Laurence Roche took over the presidency until 2002, when Mike Booth took on the position. Mike handed over the presidency in 2005 to our current President, Roy Wilson.

Our artists

Since our formation, over 330 artists have, at some time, been members of the Guild. These range from the professional artist to those who paint for leisure and have other professions, or followings, from architecture to zoologists! Many, of course, depict other subject matter as well as railway, and also combine their other interests within their railway depictions. The Guild has also been supported by 100 or more people who have joined the Friends of the Guild over the years. Most artists and Friends reside in the United Kingdom but there are a number of members who live in Europe, Canada, the USA and South Africa. Current membership stands around 170, however, even after 30 years or more, we are still finding further artists who depict subject matter within this genre.

So there it is, a potted history of the Guild of Railway Artists.

Frank Hodges,
the Chief Executive Officer

Many have asked over the years if I paint – my stock answer is always 'Yes – I do doors, windows and skirting boards.' I would not know where to start if given paints, brushes and a canvas. On that point, Lawrence Roche, one of our Past Presidents, gave me, some years ago, a painting-by-numbers kit – I still have it – unopened! However, I have learnt a lot about art. I now appreciate greatly what an artist can do. I appreciate the skill, the emotions, the creativity of all of our members, as well as other artists both past and present.

I am also asked on many occasions who is my favourite artist – the enquirer expecting the answer to be one of the notables within the Guild. Well – it's a Mr Claude Monet, GRA. or should he be a 'Fellow of the Guild'?

I have also, through the Guild, been able to travel widely throughout the country finding places previously never visited, on many occasions at the wheel of a Transit van. I like Transit vans. I have to say that motorways have been a boon and also sometimes, aggravating. They can get you from point A to B very quickly – conversely the 16 miles of roadworks at 50mph through Derbyshire in 2010 on a trip to Locomotion and back was a pain in the neck (or perhaps, thinking about it, another part of the body!).

Over this last 30 years I have also met some wonderful people – the people who run the galleries and museums we have exhibited in, who have been most helpful and accommodating, and their words at the close of the exhibition: 'It's been a very popular exhibition – our visitor figures are way higher than any of our other exhibitions.' Words I have heard from pretty well every location we have exhibited at – and being followed by 'Can you come back?'

Then there have been the visitors to the exhibitions and especially our Previews – most who marvel at the works on display and of course, some who question technical aspects of the paintings.

The world wide web has also opened up new fields of communication. This area perhaps over the last few years, with today's computerisation has been a challenge – but a most enjoyable one. I would add that this world of computers was not even in existence when the Guild was first formed – that was the days of typewriters and Gestetner duplicators. Emails had not been invented! At times I wonder whether they should have been.

This last 30 years has been a most enjoyable and rewarding journey for me. And now for some personal thanks.

First, my thanks to all members past and present for putting up with me, for their friendship, their advice and their help, which on many, if not all occasions, has been much appreciated.

My thanks also to Steve Johnson who landed me into this world of art in the first place. Unfortunately, Steve had to give up his role in the Guild due to the pressures of his day-to-day job, in 1995.

Finally, there is one more to thank and that is my wife Diana, for allowing me to indulge in this hobby, for allowing me to take over the house including the front room on many occasions for the storage of paintings in transit, and for the support given to me over the years. I think she knows how much I appreciate it.

I commend to you, the reader, this book of the 'Emotions' of the Guild's artists; the pictures within are their story. It is hoped you will enjoy the contents as much as the participants have enjoyed bringing this superb collection of railway art together.

PETER ANNABLE, GRA

Memories of Childhood

Medium: Watercolour
Size: 37.5 x 30.5cm

Like a lot of people, I find it hard to dispose of 'junk'. I still have old *Beano* annuals, *Observers Book of Birds*, football programmes etc. and amongst all of this I have a collection of old railway memorabilia.

I decided to set up a still life of some of these things which bring back fond memories of childhood.

My Dad would take me trainspotting when I was a young boy and we would take photographs with an old bellows camera, a Voigtländer. I would wait eagerly for the resulting snaps to arrive after being sent for developing and they would invariably be blurred images or locomotives half missing due to the slow shutter speed and the difficulty of lining up a moving subject.

There is also a log book of locomotives presented with the *Wizard* weekly comic, which had free photographs over a number of weeks to collect and stick in, a train ticket to Grantham from Nottingham Victoria, note books and pencil, *Trains Illustrated* and, of course, an old, battered, ABC Combined Volume from 1959.

That year was the last time that Nottingham Forest won the FA Cup. Sadly, I couldn't find room to fit the Wembley Final programme into this painting.

PETER ANNABLE, GRA

Ribblehead Viaduct

Medium: Watercolour
Size: 41.0 x 27.0cm

Situated on the beautiful 72-mile long Settle to Carlisle railway, Ribblehead Viaduct crosses the Valley of the River Ribble in North Yorkshire. It is 104 feet high and 440 yards long. Construction of the 24-arch viaduct started in 1870 and it was completed in 1874. It is now a Grade 2 listed building.

I sometimes pass the viaduct on weekends spent in Yorkshire, staying in Hawes or Ingleton and walking the Three Peaks of Whernside, Ingleborough and Penyghent. Until you stand at the side of the viaduct it is hard to appreciate the size of the structure, the hard work and skill involved in its creation, and what the navvies had to endure in this harsh environment. I have tried to capture the scene that stuck in my mind at the end of the walk over Whernside one blustery wet day, with low cloud obscuring the viaduct from the top.

As I passed the viaduct on the way to the Station Inn for some well-deserved refreshments, the rain cleared, leaving high cloud racing across the late-afternoon sky. The colour of which contrasted well with the grass in the foreground and the strong solid black limestone of the structure.

PETER ANNABLE, GRA

After the Rain

Medium: Watercolour
Size: 15.0 x 21.0cm

This watercolour of an unidentified Stanier locomotive hard at work, pulling a fast freight train, is painted using a limited palette to try to create an atmospheric study of a typical railway scene after rain. The composition is a simple one, with the positioning of the locomotive and signalbox in the bottom third of the painting, almost in silhouette, and the strong light reflecting off the wet rails, leading the eye into the picture.

I enjoy this type of painting, a direct simple, loose watercolour, using suggestion rather than detail to create a scene.

CHRIS ASHMORE, GRA

Articulated Halcyon Days

Medium: Acrylic/Acrylic ink
Size 45.0 x 32.0cm

The painting depicts the Articulated in its fantastic livery working on the California Western Railroad. The 2-6-6-2, No. 46, and 2-8-2 No. 45 have crossed the summit on the California Western and are now going to drop down to Willits as part of a double-headed excursion in June of 1974. No. 45 remains on this line while No. 46 is now at the San Diego Railroad Museum in Campo, California.

After working for many years for the Weyerhaeuser logging company and the Rayonier Inc. logging company in Washington State, the big articulated was given a new lease of life and a new livery when California Western obtained the ageing locomotive in 1969.

These were certainly the big articulated's halcyon days.

CHRIS ASHMORE, GRA

Autumn Steam

Medium: Acrylic/Acrylic ink
Size: 45.0 x 32.0cm

The painting depicts Western Maryland Shay No. 6 framed by the rusting Tygart River bridge as it prepares for a day of pulling short excursions out of Elkins depot, West Virginia. This is a particularly picturesque part of the United States of America.

The autumn fall colouring of the foliage and the rust-colour bridge framing the Lima Locomotive Works behemoth makes for a very pleasant autumn steam artistic composition. No. 6 was built for Western Maryland coal service, and was shipped to Elkins on 14 May 1945 for use on the 9 per cent grade on the Chaffe branch. It was the last Shay ever built, with a sheer mass of 162 tons, and is the largest Shay in existence.

Today, it is still like new and a spectacular example of the fine technology of geared steam locomotives.

CHRIS ASHMORE, GRA

Every young boy's dream ... a Steam Locomotive Driver

Medium: Watercolour
Size: 30.0 x 38.0cm

Could any other occupation be so charismatic as being every young boy's dream ... the driver in charge of a hissing, wheezing and steam-belching locomotive? A steam locomotive is the nearest thing man has ever created to a living thing.

Steam trains have long sparked the imagination and conjured up dreams of bygone eras.

Having driven a steam locomotive at least once a week for the last couple of years, I know the smell and the power of steam never leaves you. Most people who talk to me on the footplate always remark on the smell of the locomotive. Being the locomotive driver is a huge responsibility, but one that is certainly worth all the effort put in to get there.

My painting depicts a 'West Country' class Pacific locomotive with the firebox door open and the orange-yellow glow of the fire in the firebox illuminating the inside of the cab. The locomotive driver at the regulator surveys the rivers of steel that lay in front of him, and checking the signals ahead. Opening the regulator and checking the line is clear ... With a roar of steam from the cylinder cocks and the gentle syncopated exhaust from the chimney, the locomotive comes to life.

CHRIS ASHMORE, GRA

Steam, Smoke and Sun

Medium: Acrylic/acrylic ink
Size: 45.0 x 32.0cm

Mountain railroading at its best, as Rio Grande Nos 498 and 484 double-head, departing Alamosa in a flurry of Steam, Smoke and Sun, then heading down the three-rail track to Antonito and then over to Chama, New Mexico.

In 1961, this kind of train was a fairly regular, twice-a-week event. At Antonito both engines will take coal and water, and the helper will be needed to assist the other engines to climb the grueling 4 per cent grade to Cumbres. They were built with special valves to allow brake control between locomotives while double-heading, and were commonly found between Alamosa and Chama, They were heavily used during the pipe boom in Farmington, and hauled long freight trains between Alamosa and Farmington. Truly a railroading phenomenon.

JOHN AUSTIN, FGRA

Winter Dawn at Tamworth

Medium: Oils
Size: 76.0 x 61.0cm

The field is deserted; the 'clanger' is silent. The station cafe's not yet open. Tamworth was possibly the best-known trainspotting location in Britain in the 1950s and '60s. Stanier Pacific No. 46225 *Duchess of Gloucester,* at the time based at Crewe North, heads a London Euston to Glasgow express.

JOHN AUSTIN, FGRA

King at Night

Medium: Oils
Size: 51.0 x 40.0cm

The sight of a speeding steam engine at night, with sparks blasting into the starlit winter sky, and the glow from the firebox, combined with a snow-covered landscape, I feel provides the ultimate dramatic image for railway art.

No. 6011 *King James I* heads an express on the London to Wolverhampton main line. The Great Western 'King' class, introduced in 1927 were the most powerful 4-6-0 locomotives in Britain.

JOHN AUSTIN, FGRA

Along the Cambrian Coast

Medium: Oils
Size: 76.0 x 65.0cm

The family holidays in the 1950s, spent at Llwyngwril on the Cambrian Coast, with spectacular scenery and dramatic, ever-changing weather conditions, have inspired me to paint several pictures of this area.

Western Region 4-6-0 No. 7802 *Bradley Manor* heads south along the Cambrian Coast at Friog. The holiday location of Fairbourne is

seen in the distance, home of the Fairbourne Miniature Railway. In the far distance is Barmouth bridge, carrying the line north to Harlech and Pwllheli over the Mawddach Estuary.

Bradley Manor is one of several of the class to survive and resides on the Severn Valley Railway.

JOHN AUSTIN, FGRA

Hagley Hall on Borle Viaduct

Medium: Oils
Size: 102.0 x 76.0cm

Preserved Great Western Railway 'Hall' No. 4930 *Hagley Hall* crosses Borle Viaduct on the Severn Valley Railway, between Highley and Arley.

ERIC BOTTOMLEY, GRA

A Moment in Time

Medium: Oils
Size: 76.0 x 40.0cm

This painting was originally going to be called 'Admiration and Indifference' due to the older men admiring Sir William Stanier's masterpiece, the 'Duchess' Pacific No. 46240 *City of Coventry*, as opposed to the young boys, who, having taken the number, show no more signs of interest.

Station platforms like this were playgrounds for the hordes of trainspotters who abounded in the 1950s and '60s. It is hard to imagine now, but words of abuse and derision were shouted at locos they had already seen, whereas a new 'cop' would be greeted with cheers, as yet another number was underlined in the 'spotters' bible' the Ian Allan Combined Volume – ten shillings and sixpence's worth of temptation to spot every steam engine on British Railways at that time.

The location of the painting is fictitious, but is meant to typify any station during the days of steam where boys could get close up to the engines they sought.

As the introduction of diesel power grew apace the 'Duchesses' were to be seen on various secondary routes away from the prestigious main line, namely the routes to Birmingham New Street, Manchester London Road, Shrewsbury and that of the 'Irish Mail' along the North Wales coast to Holyhead.

My reason for painting this picture was simply the fun of re-creating memories of my very happy childhood.

GERALD BROOM, GRA

Distraction

Medium: Mixed
Size: 41.0 x 30.5cm

Perhaps the title says it all. Just another story, an image where sex is omnipresent regardless, but set within the stage of railway and landscape. Just another '45XX' dashes past the viewpoint, probably inspired by artist Philip Shepherd's 'side-on' studies. But the Acton Scott Farm Museum horses, Duke and Dragon, have long gone for pet food. The reaper binder still confuses the modern re-enactor and those that know me at Kidderminster will understand the sweet intoxication of Meggie and Sarah's 'elf shot'.

GERALD BROOM, GRA

The Midlander

Medium: Mixed
Size: 46.0 x 30.5cm

I didn't know it at the time, but it all started at one of the oldest trunk route stations in the land – the Grand Junction Railway at James Bridge, Darlaston.

In the early 1950s heaven only knows why I did not start my trainspotting in more green delights at Pleck Park only half a mile away! Perhaps, following the introduction of my peers I seemed to gravitate to this spot, set amongst the drudge and shadow of Black Country industry.

Every weekday evening at just after 8.15pm we had our own named express 'The Midlander' – ten to six off Euston, two hours Coventry, Birmingham, last stop Bescot and on to Wolverhampton, always hauled by a Bushbury 5X 'Jubilee'. Those engines became a familiar reassurance – *Atlas, Samson, Novelty, Polyphemus* – never immaculate, often late, sometimes missing, but as they dashed through that grim little station, a vision of action, the control of fire, water and air, stirred some emotion inside me that set my life's direction for ever. Visit the site today and you would never believe it ever existed – such is history.

GERALD BROOM, GRA

Lord Lichfield's Bridge *Facing page*

Medium: Mixed
Size: 56.0 x 40.0cm

There is something indefinable when walking with history. Many a quiet hour I have ambled through the Shugborough Estate and the nearby Trent and Mersey Canal around Milford.

Here, there is a lovely evocative cameo, unchanged and so typical of the railway blending into an historical landscape. Beneath the oaks and ash my mind's eye always sees a 'Nor Western' express, incidental in the background, and still I sense that social division of class.

The gamekeeper and his daughter can only gaze in deference as the Dyott family coach leaves the estate for Lichfield. Modest in comparison to Chatsworth or Blenheim, the quiet solitude of this viewpoint conveys an external magic for me as a continuity of the railways in England's history.

GERALD BROOM, GRA

The Last Summer

Medium: Mixed
Size: 206.0 x 84.0cm

It is July 1914, at Stokesay in Shropshire, overlooking the Hereford to Shrewsbury line of the joint Great Western and London & North Western railways. A southbound passenger train has just left Craven Arms, whilst plodding uphill to the Stretton gap between the Long Mynd and Ragleth Hills, is a train of Welsh steam coal.

On the lower slopes, below Stoke Wood, during a lull in the haymaking, an old gaffer, sinister in black, has ambled up to the mixed throng of rural workers. His cynical predictions in some bar room gossip are proving correct, as he indicates the passage of coal, the first of many 'Jellico Specials' for the fleet at Scapa Flow.

A young Second Lieutenant of the King's Shropshire Light Infantry dallies with his sweetheart, and in their casual innocence she toys with a poppy, unaware of the awesome future. This day is of little consequence, threatening clouds gather over the Long Mynd, and the menfolk will soon be but names on stone in Stokesay churchyard. The women will weep and continue their toil, the Onny still meanders down to Ludlow, and the seasons light and shade will forever play the hills. (Courtesy The Waterman Collection)

JONATHAN CLAY

Welsh Pony in the Aberglaslyn Pass

Medium: Oils
Size: 40.0 x 50.0cm

In my childhood and early teenage years, the Welsh Highland Railway was a distant memory, and the trackbed was my playground, a place of exploration and, later, a place for courtship! For several years we holidayed in Beddgelert, and little did I think that trains would once again run through the Aberglaslyn Pass. I've even cycled through the tunnels! In 1964 some rails and rolling stock appeared at the old Beddgelert station site, though little progress was ever made.

Now, however, the railway has been rebuilt, thanks to the efforts of the Festiniog Railway and its army of volunteers, and trains can run between Porthmadog and Carnarfon. The full story of its reconstruction can be found on the excellent web site created by the late Dr Ben Fisher. What a shame he didn't live to see it back in public service.

The painting itself was inspired by a photograph by Peter Johnson, the well-known railway journalist, author and photographer, and features Festiniog Railway George England locomotive No. 5 *Welsh Pony*. Despite some initial resistance, moves are now afoot to restore this locomotive after many decades of inactivity. Hopefully this scene can be recreated in the next few years.

JONATHAN CLAY

SNCF Locomotive 232 S 001

Medium: Gouache
Size: 42.0 x 30.0cm

I only discovered after my Dad's death that he had been in the Normandy Landings in World War II. Consequently I had no idea why we had to holiday in France in 1955, and how he knew all these French people! I now know that a lot of the places we visited in France and Belgium, such as Vimy and Ypres, were very close to his heart.

Dad was also very interested in things mechanical, an interest which I seem to have inherited, although I am nowhere near as practical as he was.

One day we were taken to a railway station (which I now know to be Lille) where we spent the day taking photographs of the trains. One of the locomotives he photographed was a huge streamliner. This I discovered was one of a small number of prototypes built just before the war and represented the zenith of French locomotive development, only the 241Ps being more powerful.

I have used Dad's photograph to depict No. 232 S 001 as one of my well-known 'Locomotive Portraits', which I have been producing for the last twelve years or so, and which now cover over 600 subjects. This format, of a locomotive on its own, with no background, has been very good to me over the years. Sadly, the locomotive no longer exists, although a slightly larger version, No. 232 U 001 is in the French National Railway Museum at Mulhouse.

JONATHAN CLAY

Ashe Street in the Rain, Tralee & Dingle Railway

Medium: Oils
Size: 76.0 x 51.0cm

From an early age I was a confirmed narrow gauge railway enthusiast. In the late 1950s there was little available in the terms of literature, but I did possess an Oakwood Press book of narrow gauge railways from which I learnt that all the lines in Ireland had long since closed. As a result it never occurred to me that I would ever see the Tralee & Dingle Railway.

Fast forward to the early 1990s: Barbara and I had for several years taken a few days holiday each year touring Southern Ireland. On one of these tours we ended up in Tralee one evening and stayed in a splendid hotel. The intention was to explore the 'T&D' the following day.

As we set out for the Dingle peninsular we came across a railway platform complete with train. The locomotive (T&D No. 5) was in steam and coupled to two coaches of rather Continental appearance. We had to go for a ride. Although the recreated line is only a couple of miles long it was a spooky experience, particularly as the coach contained some of the very photographs I had seen all those years ago. It was definitely a 'hairs on the back of the neck' moment.

We later stood at the summit of the line, overlooking Dingle, and I swear I could hear a train coming – or maybe it was the wind! Sadly, at the moment the railway is not running and looks decidedly run-down.

JONATHAN CLAY

Duke of Gloucester at Speed

Medium: Gouache
Size: 42.0 x 30.0cm

Although a narrow gauge fan, if I am asked to name my favourite locomotive it has to be *Duke of Gloucester*. In my trainspotting days by the West Coast Main Line I don't think I ever saw it. However, I did think it looked right! It was only in later years that it emerged that it was never really developed properly, and it was even suggested that parts of it were incorrectly constructed.

I first saw the locomotive, or rather the constituent parts of it, spread around the yard and shed at Loughborough on the Great Central Railway in the mid-1970s. Then, it was dubbed 'Project Impossible'. But as we all know, the impossible sometimes happens and in 1986 it was restored to steam. Since then it has constantly been improved and has worked many times on the main line very successfully.

The painting itself is a 'homage'. My artistic influences as a child were Frank Wootton, Paul B. Mall and most importantly George Heiron. His famous picture of *Britannia* at speed was on my wall for years as a child, and I collected all the front covers of *Model Railway News* which he illustrated. Over the years I have collected many books with his pictures in and he remains my hero, though sadly he is no longer with us. Here is my attempt to recreate this picture – but with my favourite locomotive.

MATTHEW COUSINS, GRA

St Pancras Poster

Medium: Gouache
Size: 30.0 x 40.0cm

I was asked to create a poster that would portray both the modern and historical aspects of the renovated St Pancras International station.

When I visited the station I was very impressed with the light feeling of the renovated roof and so set this as the sky background. The beauty of the original hotel building is fascinating. I also decided that the imaginary train would pass back through time from today's Eurostar, through InterCity, 'Blue Pullman', British Railways Mark 1, LMS and Midland coaches, to the earliest days of the original station.

MATTHEW COUSINS, GRA

Coronation

Medium: Gouache
Size: 49.0 x 30.0cm

The LNER poster for the 'Coronation' showed a very well-painted landscape but did not portray the train very well. So in this creation the artist has taken a real setting just north of the Border in summer when the train would have got there late in the day from King's Cross.

MATTHEW COUSINS, GRA

Cock o' the North over the Forth

Medium: Gouache
Size: 30.0 x 39.0cm

I wanted to combine the two images of the Forth Bridge and Sir Nigel Gresley's magnum opus *Cock o' the North*, which was built specifically for the Edinburgh–Aberdeen route over the Firth of Forth. I have portrayed the scene in late afternoon/early evening light, which I think gives a suitably dramatic scene for the two iconic railway masterpieces.

John Cowley, GRA

The 'Decadian'

Medium: Oils
Size: 56.0 x 46.0cm

Sheffield Park in East Sussex became the home and prototype for preservation railways and now hosts many fine locos. The GWR 'Dukedog' 4-4-0, No. 3217 *Earl of Berkeley* was just one of a dozen or so engines at the Bluebell Railway when it was chosen to display the tenth year anniversary headboard.

In those heady days such celebrations were much more informal and the scene depicted here in 1970 shows plainly that Health and Safety Executive power was still to be realised. Whilst happy to paint preservation scenes, it is those gritty shed days that inspire me most. However, while living very close to this line I did spend many glorious early mornings videoing the firing and preparation in the yard.

FREDERICK C.B. COX

Last Day of Steam

Medium: Oils
Size: 60.0 x 40.0cm

With rust, dirt and grime evident of the demise of the steam era, sadly those engines still in use were in a deplorable state, not having seen a cleaner, probably in months. The painting emphasises these conditions synonymous with the forthcoming closures.

The shed yard too was neglected, with debris strewn around and piles of ash everywhere. The Fairburn 2-6-4 tank engine, No. 42063, gently simmers on the shed road, awaiting the attention of the engine crew, just arriving to start what will be their final shift.

IAN DOCWRA

Shap Snow

Medium: Oils
Size: 25.0 x 30.0cm

The scene is a stunning winter's day near Scout Green, on the climb to Shap Summit, with a heavy northbound freight train grinding up the hill behind an unidentified 8F, banked by a BR Class 4, 4-6-0.

My father took my mother and me to Shap bank on several occasions in 1967 and 1968, and I remember the succession of labouring northbound steam trains, and the equally untroubled descending southbound workings. He took much cine film footage of the activity, which lives on to preserve the memories.

IAN DOCWRA

Ashtead, Summer 1959

Medium: Oils
Size: 35.0 x 22.0cm

An idyllic summer's day in Surrey. A Victoria to Portsmouth express, led by 6-PAN unit No. 3022, heads south through Ashtead station, near Epsom. The only buildings still standing in this scene today are the houses behind the southbound platform station buildings.

My parents and I moved to Ashtead in 1981, long after the station buildings had been replaced by ugly BR modular constructions, rising-arm level crossing barriers, and colour light signals.

MICHAEL FLANDERS

City of Coventry, Perth 1955

Medium: Oils
Size: 60.0 x 50.0cm

City of Coventry, engine No. 46240, is a busy little scene. The focal point of the painting is the workman cleaning the boiler of ash. The figure is clearly using the shovel to open the hot boiler door. I find the human element in any painting hugely important to give scale and add life to the image, which in turn also tells a story.

The ash trucks to the left form an important part of the composition as they help lead the eye into the painting, past the engine and onto the coal tower in the distance thus creating depth. Framed by the dark trucks, smoke and clouds this makes the burgundy engine stand proud in the painting.

City of Coventry was an LMS 'Coronation' class 4-6-2 locomotive, built in 1940 and was withdrawn from service in 1964.

MICHAEL FLANDERS

On the Turntable

Medium: Oils
Size: 115.0 x 76.0cm

'On the Turntable' was inspired by the extreme contrast of light and dark coupled with the grime of Leeds Holbeck shed, where the struggle to turn engine No. 45574 (named *India*) would have been a regular challenge for the workmen. When painting the figures I can't help but think about how the conditions and work would impact on their lives.

The figures were a key part of this painting, giving an idea of scale and weight to the engine. Further drama was created by the light and shade within the painting. India was a Stanier-designed 'Jubilee' class 4-6-0. Built in 1934 it was disposed of in 1966.

RAY GALE

Tramways of Vienna

Medium: Silk Screen
Size: 42.0 x 34.0cm

The magic of Vienna is expressed by its architecture, art museums, and tramway system, passing the famous Ringstrasse and giant Ferris Wheel, to experiencing the Konzerte im Kursalon Wien.

Tramway sketches were made in Vienna in 2008, and the ensuing print made as a 'one-off', as it incorporated a single different technique of painterly effect. A variety of coloured screen inks were laid on the paper surface, and then squeezed through as normal practice. Continuing with a stopping-out process of the screen surface, and paper-cut stencils, the process finished with a photo-stencil of the original pen-and-ink drawing in two colours, slightly off-set to create a 3D effect.

RAY GALE

Didcot Steam Centre

Medium: Silk screen
Size: 36.0 x 22.5cm

An interior of contrasts: the bold and heavy machinery dwarfed by this refined period carriage, painted in attractive Great Western colours.

A notebook sketch of one hour, five minutes was made in situ. The drawing in black ballpoint pen was not changed in size, but redrawn in pen-and-ink onto drafting film, and then used in the master drawing, from which the paper stencils were cut, finishing with a photo-stencil of the ink drawing.

A photo-stencil is made by exposing the drawing with stencil film in a light-box for two minutes, then washing out the film, leaving a negative image, through which the ink is passed, giving the positive, original line drawing, in any colour required.

RAY GALE

Passing by

Medium: Silk Screen
Size: 47.5 x 34.0cm

Seen from a South Western train travelling between Mortlake and Barnes stations are these allotments, bordered by the railway lines and a very neat colourful row of cottages, which in their own right are an artist's delight, but my view had to be seen looking back from the cottages towards the railway.

Electric-powered trains are not a popular subject, but with the diverse liveries now appearing, the artist and general public may find the vision enlightening.

This print used a stopping-out process, paper-cut stencils and a photo-stencil of the original pen-and-ink drawing, and was drawn in situ.

41

MIKE GUNNELL, AGAvA, GRA

Journey into the Unknown

Medium: Chromacolour
Size: 32.6 x 23.3cm

The sight of small children standing on platforms, clutching their suitcases and gas masks, being sent off alone to an unknown (for them) destination, will never be forgotten. The evacuation of children of Autumn 1939, proved in the event to be unnecessary as the bombing of London and other large cities did not happen, but it proved to be a vital rehearsal for the real thing in the summer of 1940.

In my painting, the faces of the children in the group waiting to board the train show a variety of emotions. Fear and uncertainty of what they would find at their destination, mingled with trepidation about the journey and the worry of meeting so many strangers in close contact on the train.

Some stand straight and tall showing courage, perhaps with a touch of bravado, others have a sad, almost haunted look, which may stem from their forced separation from their families. One child clings to her precious doll for comfort.

The more I learn about the evacuation, the more thankful I am that I had already been taken away by my parents from the danger zone. I was only three at the height of the blitz on Hull. I derive great pleasure from using the sepia chromacolour to evoke the atmosphere of the era when black and white photography reigned supreme and colour was a rarity. It enables me to express through the human form, story and emotion.

MIKE GUNNELL, AGAvA, GRA

Happy Carefree Holidays

Medium: Chromacolour
Size: 20.8 x 29.5cm

The art of the railway poster has fascinated me for the last twenty years, in general, those influenced by the Art Deco movement and in particular, the poster art of Tom Purvis produced for the LNER. His was a minimalistic style of painting with interlocking shapes, flat primary colours and the elimination of detail. It conveys the carefree atmosphere of the seaside of the late 1920s.

'Happy Carefree Holidays' is not as sparsely painted as a Purvis poster but still retains the image created by interlocking shapes. The painting is intended to depict those carefree holiday times, which evoked such happy memories in generations of people. The girls are enjoying the sensory pleasures of warm sunshine on their faces, a light ozone-laden breeze caressing their bodies, the cool water splashing their legs, and the sand firm beneath their feet. It is a vision of human joy.

The Ocean Coast was the name created by the Great Western Railway Publicity Department to describe 1,000 miles of ever-varying scenery from Dorset to North Wales.

NICK HARDCASTLE, MA(RCA), GRA

Vauxhall Station

Medium: Watercolour
Size: 54.0 x 37.0cm

My regular commute into Central London some years ago involved using Vauxhall station in South London.

One day, I came home earlier than usual and was struck by the dramatic light caused by the late afternoon sun. Normally, the station was quite gloomy, almost Dickensian, so to see it bathed in sunlight was quite a revelation. I went back the following day and took some photographs and made some pencil sketches on the spot.

For me it is an extremely evocative painting, full of atmosphere and drama.

NICK HARDCASTLE, MA(RCA), GRA

Oliver Cromwell with an express in East Anglia in the 1950s

Medium: Watercolour
Size: 41.0 x 30.0cm

This painting was produced as a commission – but one I enjoyed doing. The client wished to have a typical East Anglian main line scene set in the mid-1950s featuring 'Britannia' class No. 70013 *Oliver Cromwell* at speed on an express.

I think it conveys the thrill of witnessing a powerful steam locomotive in its prime, working hard, on a cold winter's day with the low sun glinting off the side of the engine as it speeds past.

JOHN HARDY, GRA

Imminent Departure

Medium: Acrylic
Size: 39.0 x 28.0cm

The artist states that the intention of this
imagined view of somewhere on the Western
Region is to show some of the infrastructure of
the steam age, most of which has been swept
away. He adds that, thankfully, a number of
such scenes were saved or recreated on heritage
railways, to be enjoyed today.

45

JOHN HARRISON, ATD, GRA

Shimmering Rails

Medium: Watercolour
Size: 49.0 x 33.5cm

The train has departed, but the glinting tracks and junctions remain – a lifelong source of fascination for me. Shining rails have an added appeal when seen at sunset or by night and are a constant source of inspiration for my paintings.

The scene which I have tried to recapture in this painting was familiar to me in my boyhood – Rainford Junction station in South West Lancashire. In those days a constant stream of traffic, from loose-coupled goods to cross-Pennine expresses between Liverpool Exchange and West Yorkshire via the ex-L&Y Calder Valley route, headed down the main line. The bay platforms on the right were for branch trains to Skelmersdale and Ormskirk, while the curves to the left carried the push-pull train to stations at Rainford, Rookery, Mill Lane, Crank, Moss Bank and St Helens Shaw St. I travelled this line from Moss Bank to Rainford many times with my parents in the 1930s and '40s in an elderly two-coach set hauled by a LNWR coal tank.

Now the branches and sidings have all gone and the main line towards Liverpool is but a single track with an hourly DMU between Wigan Wallgate and Kirkby.

JOHN HARRISON, ATD, GRA

Wet Night in Liverpool

Medium: Watercolour
Size: 48.0 x 34.0cm

In the early 1950s I spent five happy years at the Liverpool Regional College of Art in Hope Street. The tram tracks and junctions around the city always held a special fascination for me, particularly when the tracks and sets glistened under the street lights on a wet evening. Although the conversion programme from tram to bus had already begun, numerous complicated track junctions were still in full use around the city.

The junction shown in this painting of Islington Square still carried seven tram routes. I sometimes stood on this corner in my lunch hour, watching the trams negotiate the various curves. By the '50s most city centre tracks were asphalt paved but the old traditional sets, shown here, gave much greater scope for the artist or photographer and the yellow sodium street lights created a wonderful atmosphere on a misty damp evening.

JOHN HARRISON, ATD, GRA

Smoke and Steam at Bank Quay

Medium: Watercolour
Size: 50.5 x 35.0cm

Smoke, steam, mist and fog were very much a part of my younger years in Lancashire. In those days the towns and cities of the North were, without doubt, smoky dirty places, yet, I still feel some nostalgia for those times. I have frequently conjured up memories from the smoky past as the subject matter for my paintings – but I have no desire to return to the smoke and grime, now thankfully gone for ever.

In this painting I have tried to recapture memories of Bank Quay station, Warrington – still a Lancashire town in those days. The trains which I recall with special affection were the so-called 'Manchester Club Trains', one of which I have depicted here. The club trains, which ran until the 1960s, were a hang-over from a former age when Manchester businessmen who lived on the North Wales and Fylde coasts commuted daily by rail. These trains seemed to keep alive memories of the London & North Western and Lancashire & Yorkshire railways, and even though they carried no locomotive headboards still managed to retain an air of distinction with smart-looking coaches and locomotives.

JOHN HARRISON, ATD, GRA

Settle to Carlisle, 2010

Medium: Watercolour
Size: 53.5 x 34.5cm

I first became acquainted with the Settle to Carlisle line in the 1960s and '70s when the Class 45 'Peak' diesels still held sway. Since then I have followed its fluctuating fortunes closely, mourning for its near extinction and rejoicing in its more recent resurgence as depicted here. I have travelled the line on numerous occasions and also followed its course closely from every negotiable by-road. Fortunately, one of our daughters lives in the Eden Valley close by.

This scene encapsulates the modern S&C – a working railway dominated by container and hopper traffic. An EWS (now DB Schenker) hopper train approaches Ais Gill Summit, as seen from the B6259 road north of the Moor Cock Inn. I must confess that I now prefer to paint from the comfort of my home, so this painting is based on some of the many photographs I have taken along the S&C route over the years. Even though it may not be wind-blown and rain-spattered, I hope that it still manages to capture a little of the S&C magic.

PHILIP D. HAWKINS, FGRA

Passing the Can

Medium: Oils
Size: 25.5 x 30.5cm

An ex-Midland Railway Johnson 0-6-0 No. 58170 slumbers in a quiet backwater whilst the driver hands down the all-important 'mash can' for refuelling.

These ancient 'fivers', as we called them, were a constant presence during my childhood when I would watch them struggling and wheezing up the embankment at the back of our home in Winson Green, Birmingham. They were usually Monument Lane or Bescot-allocated engines and to my young eyes they looked really ancient, indeed they were. Introduced as a class in 1875, No. 58170 was one of a batch introduced in 1917. Many lasted well into British Railways' days.

PHILIP D. HAWKINS, FGRA

Saltley Winter

Medium: Oils
Size: 30.5 x 25.5cm

A Stanier 8F 2-8-0 battles through the bitter winter of 1962/63 past the entrance to Saltley engine sheds with a southbound freight train.

After 'bunking' Saltley sheds we would settle down at the entrance (the shed 'throat' in railway parlance) to watch traffic on the busy ex-Midland Railway line from Birmingham New Street to Derby and freight trains passing by to and from Washwood Heath marshalling yards. Freight trains heading south, as in 'Saltley Winter', would often require the assistance of a banking engine for the climb from Saltley to King's Heath along the Camp Hill line.

PHILIP D. HAWKINS, FGRA

Tyseley Roundhouse

Medium: Oils
Size: 35.5 x 25.5cm

A bedraggled ex-Great Western Railway Collett 0-6-2T, No. 5658 balances on the turntable inside one of Tyseley's roundhouses in the early 1960s.

From the age of ten I lived in Acocks Green, Birmingham, which happened to be just a ten minute bike ride from Tyseley engine sheds. Needless to say, this became a well-cycled route from 1959 to 1962 with the result that the shed and its varied locomotive allocation became very familiar to me. Quite often a rare engine, a source of great excitement in those days, would be lurking inside one of the two roundhouses. No. 5658, not a rarity, but a Tyseley resident for many years, was one of three or four such engines allocated for local freight work and would occasionally find themselves on a local passenger service. To simply stand and stare, absorbing the wonderfully unique atmosphere of a working steam locomotive depot was the inspiration to recreate such a scene on canvas.

PHILIP D. HAWKINS, FGRA

All Engines Must Stop

Medium: Oils
Size: 51.0 x 41.0cm

A 'Castle' class 4-6-0, No. 5045 *Earl of Dudley*, is seen amongst the evocative paraphernalia of steam days at Wolverhampton Stafford Road engine sheds, c1960.

Stafford Road was the first non-Birmingham engine shed that I visited, somewhere around 1958. This scene, showing the coaling stage and turntable, was about a quarter of a mile from the actual depot. With a buddy or two I would sit on a tatty grass bank, enjoying the contents of our duffle bags, and watch the to and fro of such magnificent machines as 'Castles' and 'Kings', as well as lesser mortals, to our hearts' content. Such an everyday event at the time, but what would we give to witness such happenings today?

PHILIP D. HAWKINS, FGRA

Leander on the Lickey

Medium: Oils
Size: 76.0 x 51.0cm

William Stanier's 'Jubilee' class 4-6-0s were a constant presence during my formative years in Birmingham. Indeed, from my home in Winson Green the Bushbury-allocated members of the class could be seen on a daily basis but, at New Street station 'Jubes' from many other parts of the London Midland Region were regular visitors, including those allocated to Bristol Barrow Road engine sheds. The likes of *Trafalgar*, *Shovell*, *Barfleur* and *Leander* would arrive on trains from the West Country to the North including the 'Devonian'. To see and hear these handsome engines really working, a visit to the Lickey Bank was a must.

In my painting, No. 45690 *Leander* has almost reached the summit with the northbound 'Devonian', c1959.

CHRIS HOLLAND, GRA

Garsdale Troughs

Medium: Gouache
Size: 53.0 x 37.0cm

The Settle & Carlisle line has an unenviable reputation for bad weather conditions, but I think that sometimes they actually add something to the picture, when you consider that the line was built in such inhospitable wilderness. Incomparable, stunning, breathtaking, dramatic and unrivalled are the superlatives that have been used to describe its scenic qualities.

The scene I chose is the water troughs at Garsdale, the highest in Great Britain. The locomotive, rebuilt 'Patriot' 4-6-0 No. 45530 *Sir Frank Ree*, was the final survivor of its class, lasting until December 1965.

If you feel you need to put on a coat and put up your umbrella while looking at this picture, then I have done my job.

And to think that some politicians actually tried to close this line! How true the words of Oscar Wilde were, when he said of such: 'They know the price of everything and the value of nothing.' 'Well done' to those who fought to save it – and succeeded.

CHRIS HOLLAND, GRA

Grace and Grandeur

Medium: Acrylic
Size: 76.0 x 51.0cm

Gresley A3 Pacific No. 60082 *Neil Gow* heads the up 'Thames–Clyde Express' the last few miles to the summit at Ais Gill on the Settle & Carlisle line. The title I gave to the picture refers to the graceful appearance of the locomotive in a setting of wild grandeur. The hill in the background is Wild Boar Fell.

In the '60s, nine ex-LNER A3s were unexpectedly allocated to Holbeck shed and were only diagrammed for working north of Leeds. They were in the hands of drivers and firemen brought up on LMS engines, but nevertheless they took to them very well indeed. I also took to these engines and just had to include one in my selection, along with what is one of the bleakest but most beautiful locations.

CHRIS HOLLAND, GRA

Edinburgh Waverley

Medium: Acrylic
Size: 76.0 x 51.0cm

The scene here is of the west end of Edinburgh Waverley station. From left to right an A3 Pacific is just leaving with a northbound express; standing on the platform awaiting 'Right of Way' is an Al Pacific on an express, while in the background is an unidentified locomotive adding its contribution to the smoky atmosphere. Finally, the rear end of a J83 0-6-0T on empty stock can be seen.

The view point above the Mound Tunnel not only gives us a vista of the station, but

Princes Street Gardens, the North British Hotel, and some other notable sights of Edinburgh. Together with the 'mish-mash' of railway lines, these all combine to make a picture which keeps your interest, and one I found enjoyable to paint.

CHRIS HOLLAND, GRA

No. 2 Roundhouse, Holbeck

Medium: Gouache
Size: 53.0 x 37.0cm

My selection had to include a shed scene of Leeds Holbeck. The depot was one of the sheds which over the latter years of steam received much attention from enthusiasts and photographers who wanted to capture the magic of the atmosphere, as light and shade played upon the movement of smoke and steam. Coupled with a great variety of motive power, all elements combine to make a very atmospheric picture.

On the left is a Fairburn tank No. 42052, in the centre is preserved Midland Kirtley Class 156 No. 158A, which is part of the National Collection. The 'Black 5', No. 44767, was unique among the 842 members of the class as it was the only one to be fitted with Stephenson link motion and is also preserved.

Some people say of my work 'I can smell the smoke' or 'It reminds me of hot oil' and so on, in which case I have achieved what I set out to do, which is to record something which no longer exists. The steam shed was demolished in 1970.

JOHN HUGHES, GRA

Great Western Essence

Medium: Acrylic
Size: 42.0 x 26.0cm

This scene typifies what is disparagingly called 'God's Wonderful Railway', for me this is exactly what it was. Now, you may prefer a majestic 'King' with 14 coaches rushing off to Bristol, or a 28XX with a hundred 10-ton wagons performing herculean feats, but I think the rural branch line is the epitome of the GWR. The unhurried trundle down some bucolic byway, the leisurely pause at some quiet village station, the friendly chat between passengers and staff, and in the background the wheezing and snuffles of the little engine. Then the signal falls, a toot on the whistle, and with a singular lack of urgency the train wanders off into the distance. Quiet returns to this bastion of Englishness and a porter shuffles down the platform to share a cup of tea with the signalman.

Now is this reality or myth – I know what I think.

JOHN HUGHES, GRA

Phoenix

Medium: Acrylic
Size: 33.0 x 21.0cm

In the late 1950s I visited the site of the old Welsh Highland Railway with the idea of photographing some of the remains. With my family we walked some of the trackbed including the tunnels at the Aberglasllyn Pass. I visualised how grand it must have looked when it was working and returned to it many times. Then a silly rumour – there were plans to reopen the line. I really wanted to see this but wondered if it would happen in my lifetime – and last year it did; *extraordinary!*

JOHN HUGHES, GRA

Just in Time

Medium: Acrylic
Size: 41.0 x 26.0cm

Anticipating an afternoon at the shops the young ladies hurry to catch the train. The morning rain clouds are moving off and sunshine is promised for the rest of the day. The driver smiles, he has noticed them run along the platform, heard the excited chatter and giggles, and senses the exuberance, then remembers he was young once.

JOHN HUGHES, GRA

River Mist

Medium: Acrylic
Size: 48.0 x 33.0cm

Approaching Golant station along the River Fowey, a beautiful setting for a ubiquitous auto train. River and railway often create pleasing scenes for an artist who, with a little luck, can make a pleasant painting, but add a little mist and the effect can be magical.

JOHN HUGHES, GRA

The End

Medium: Acrylic
Size: 38.0 x 37.0cm

An epitaph for a railway I knew and loved.
It was inefficient, uneconomic, dirty, and I
thought it was wonderful. I miss it very much.

BERNARD JONES, NDD. ATC. GRA

Redhill Station, December 1964

Medium: Oils
Size: 51.0 x 41.0cm

During my time at art school and college in the early '60s I and a number of fellow students were employed on a casual basis at Redhill station during the two weeks run-up to Christmas. Redhill was unusual in having a GPO Sorting Office on the station site and during the Christmas period extra labour was required (actually by British Railways). The work involved loading and unloading mail bags on and off trains, both local electrics and mail trains from London, which ran into the GPO siding.

My painting is based on a black and white photograph which I took at the beginning of the morning shift at around 6.30am on a cold and frosty morning. The camera was an Ilford Sportsman 35mm – a 21st birthday present that year.

Although Redhill was situated on the London–Brighton main line, which was electric, there was a small steam shed there to service locomotives working the Reading and Tonbridge lines. My photograph did not show a locomotive, but I have incorporated a Bulleid 'Q1 class 0-6-0 coming off shed, wreathed in steam. A vision I clearly remember.

BERNARD JONES, NDD. ATC. GRA

The 'Ulster Express' departing Euston

Medium: Oils
Size: 51.0 x 41.0cm

During my childhood in Surrey my family and I spent many summers in Ireland, staying on a small farm where my mother grew up, in Co. Tyrone. The journey to Ireland was something of an adventure involving mostly train travel. The longest part of the journey was from London Euston to Heysham in Lancashire from which, at that time, a passenger ferry sailed to Belfast.

Growing up in Horley, Surrey, meant that I did not see a great deal of steam activity as the London–Brighton main line was electrified in the 1930s and the electric multiple units were not too inspiring.

I have depicted in this work, the 'Ulster Express', which connected with the Heysham ferries, leaving Euston in the late afternoon and climbing Camden Bank. I clearly remember the atmosphere of the 'old' Euston station, the whistles, exhaust blasts and the pervading smells of coal smoke, hot oil and decaying fish!

WYNNE B. JONES GRA

When I grow up....

Medium: Pencil sketch
Size: 17.0 x 24.0cm

Inspiration for this sketch came from childhood memories when the promise by my parents of an imminent holiday to Yorkshire (my mother's birthplace) resulted in my older brother and me being gripped with excitement as the big day approached. The journey in those days from North Wales to the West Riding of Yorkshire was quite a trek, involving several bus and train journeys until we finally reached our destination of Skipton in the early evening.

I can recall standing on the platform of Wrexham General station eagerly awaiting the arrival of our first train which inevitably, would feature the driver leaning out of the cab window as the engine thundered in and then came to a gradual halt in front of us. How I longed, like most schoolboys at that time, to be a train driver!

My sketch shows the loco driver in typical pose at the controls of BR Standard Class 5 4-6-0 No: 73054. This engine was built in 1954 and was allocated to the London Midland Region and operated out of Bath and Bristol, and also saw service on the Crewe to Shrewsbury line via Nantwich and Whitchurch.

WYNNE B. JONES GRA

Great Orme Tramway Terminus, Llandudno, North Wales

Medium: Oils
Size: 60.0 x 40.0cm

Having been born and brought up in North Wales during the post-war era of the 1950s, Llandudno, together with Rhyl, were arguably

the two most popular holiday destinations on the North Wales coast at that time.

Visits to Llandudno by steam train always induced a high level of anticipation and excitement and I have always been intrigued by the Great Orme trams. Opened on 31 July 1902, this is the only cable-hauled tramway operating on British public roads. At its summit (679ft), on a clear day the Great Orme offers panoramic views of Anglesey to the west, the Isle of Man to the north, Blackpool and the Lake District to

the north east and Snowdonia National Park to the south.

I've harboured a desire to depict the tram system in some form or other for a number of years, and the opportunity has finally arrived. My painting is a contemporary view of the tramway terminus with distant views eastwards between the terminus canopy and the middle distance buildings, and hopefully highlights the contrast between Edwardian innovation and modern day technology.

WYNNE B. JONES GRA

Giants at Rest

Medium: Oils
Size: 41.0 x 31.0cm

Steam sheds are the perfect subject matter for the railway artist, and with its cathedral and ethereal qualities, York roundhouse, which now forms part of the National Railway Museum, provides the perfect backdrop to my painting. This features a scene during the late 1950s. Left to right are York stalwart Q6 class 0-8-0 No. 63344, shed visitors Peppercorn Class A1 4-6-2 No. 60152 *Holyrood* and Riddles BR Class 9F 2-10-0 No. 92000, all awaiting their next duties.

66

WYNNE B. JONES GRA

Hyperion – Over the Forth

Medium: Oils
Size: 50 x 40cm

The Forth railway bridge, the world's first major steel bridge, ranks as one of the great engineering feats of the Victorian era. Designed by Sir John Fowler and Benjamin Baker, and completed on 4 March 1890, the bridge, Scotland's biggest Listed Building, forms a vital link in Network Rail's East Coast railway system.

Eminent painters such as Terence Cuneo and David Shepherd have produced work featuring the Forth Bridge and this inspired me to paint this picture which features Gresley A3 Pacific No. 60037 *Hyperion* with a southbound Edinburgh express, steaming over the bridge in the late 1950s.

MORGAN LEWIS

Function and Beauty

Medium: Oils
Size: 76.0 x 63.5cm

Inspired by the powerful magic created by old cowboy films and the vast wild North American Rocky Mountains, the picture depicts one of the final freight movements on the Rio Grande Southern (RGS) in September 1951.

K27 class Mikado No. 461 is hauling a string of empty double-deck stock cars due to be loaded with sheep for grazing on the summer pastures at Lizard Head, elevation 10,250ft.

The RGS was one of the 3ft gauge railways built in Colorado Rocky Mountains and was similar to the Durango & Silverton which is currently operated as a tourist line. The part of the RGS depicted is between Ophir and Lizard Head, and is of particular interest due to the difficult terrain and the need for many spectacular wooden trestle bridges.

MORGAN LEWIS

Clouds, Smoke and Sunshine

Medium: Oils
Size: 101.0 x 76.5cm

The picture expresses a desire to offer an alternative style that is simplified and bold. It shows an ex. works, ex-Great Western Railway 'Hall' class locomotive, with a through freight, climbing Sapperton Bank, Gloucestershire, in the early 1960s.

The clouds have been emphasised so they are a dominant feature and colours are intensified to enhance the impression of distance and vibrancy.

KEVIN PARRISH

Tornado

Medium: Oils
Size: 60.0 x 45.0cm

This is Kevin's tribute to the people involved with the Al Locomotive Trust for completing the 50th Al class locomotive, No. 60163 *Tornado*, in 2008, after the previous 49 were scrapped with the demise of steam in 1968. He has been inspired by their achievement, to create this image.

His interest in the Al Pacifics goes back to his childhood and it is a joy for him to know that we now have, once again, a representative of this great steam locomotive class, originally designed by Mr A. H. Peppercorn.

KEVIN PARRISH

Waiting for the Train

Medium: Oils
Size: 65.0 x 40.0cm

A memory of New Street station, Birmingham, as it was in the early 1960s prior to its demolition in 1965. Kevin says that he remembers as a child, standing on Platform 10 (depicted here) with his parents, waiting for the train to arrive. It was a draughty, cold wait, and the train was late!

This image was first shown at a local model railway exhibition to seek comments on the work. The painting provoked a strong, emotional reaction from the public. Many said how his image brought back fond memories of waiting on the platform, with its beautiful arched roof dating back to 1884, and that it should never have been demolished. A few people remembered how they witnessed the destruction of the station with a ball and chain by workmen at the time, and how it was a heart-breaking experience for them.

How life was at a slower pace in those days, with the railway staff, with their hands in pockets, having time for a chat on the platform when there were train delays.

What a typical scene this was at the time. The image depicts a 'Jubilee' class locomotive, patiently waiting on the inner track, ready to be assigned to a passenger train.

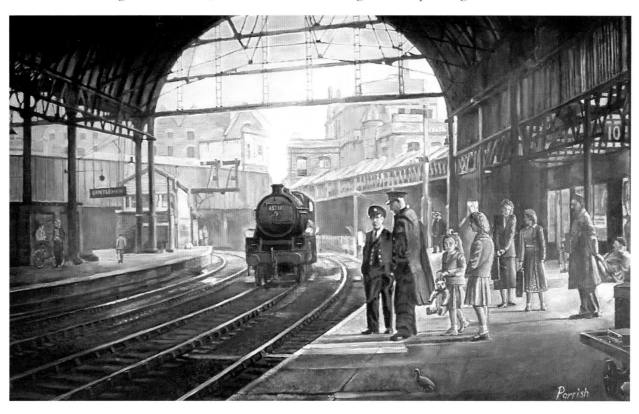

BRIAN ROBINSON

Early Shift

Medium: Acrylic
Size: 42.0 x 38.0cm

Based just outside Manchester, Newton Heath MPD on the Leeds line, was run by British Rail until its demolition in 1969. The painting depicts an industrial-type 0-6-0 saddle tank on shunting duty in a shed yard in the early morning, with a 'Black Five' 4-6-0 in the background, and a hint of the carriage works in the distance. Using some artistic licence, the intention was to illustrate the everyday railway yard environment that working people at that time would have been familiar with. The locos were photographed by Brian on preserved sites, and the background was based on archive reference material of Newton Heath MPD.

BRIAN ROBINSON

Side-lined

Medium: Watercolour
Size: 30.0 x 35.0cm

In an area near Manchester, bound on three sides by main lines and forming a triangle, was a yard and motive power depot known as Patricroft. During the decline of the steam era in the 1960s there was a gradual increase in the amount of rolling stock that was placed in sidings and yards and allowed to decay. This painting is set at the beginning of this period, showing two brakevans no longer required, parked in the yard.

BRIAN ROBINSON

End of the Line

Medium: Acrylic
Size: 62.0 x 43.0cm

After the Second World War the local cement works in West Thurrock in Essex, near where I lived as a boy, relied on the local quarry for its supply of chalk which was hauled up through a cutting in the chalk, out of the quarry and across the local main road (no gates, just a man with a flag!). The locomotives used were 0-6-0 saddle and pannier tanks of various vintages, usually in rather poor condition. During the late 1950s the quarry and railway fell into disuse and for a few years after, locos and odds and ends of rolling stock could be found in spurs and sidings, neglected and overgrown with vegetation. This is a painting of how I remember it.

To create the picture I used my own photographs of a preserved saddle tank and rolling stock that I photographed in Suffolk and combined them with my own memories of the area at the time.

MALCOLM ROOT, FGRA

Gresley Gold

Medium: Oils
Size: 60.5 x 45.5cm

The painting depicts a Class V2 class 2-6-2 locomotive designed by Sir Nigel Gresley and introduced in 1936. The three-cylinder design was very successful, particularly during the war. It was equally at home working both passenger and freight trains.

There is a certain nostalgia for me in painting a rear view of a locomotive, as this was a view often seen from the platform when, like a lot of other boys from that era, I used to watch trains.

Engines often tend to be dark and dirty subjects to paint. I however love colour. Any opportunity to introduce bright colours into a painting is a welcome one. The setting sun often produces spectacular light effects, which allow me to indulge in my love of colour.

As regards location – it can be anywhere your imagination takes you!

MALCOLM ROOT, FGRA

Liverpool Street EC2

Medium: Oils
Size: 76.0 x 61.0cm

Over the years an artist develops his or her style of painting, which means that occasionally early works can differ somewhat in their appearance. Although painted in 1982 I have included this picture because it was one I was very fond of and because it helped me secure my Full Membership of the Guild of Railway Artists.

Liverpool Street EC2, the setting for this picture, was always a dirty, sooty place with many train movements and locomotives awaiting their next turn of duty. When we were lucky enough to go to London we travelled by train and this is a typical scene that would have greeted us in the late 1950s.

It was inevitable that later on in life this image would be committed to canvas. Although not immediately apparent in the reproduction, I remember painting some very bright colours into the heaps of ash which I was very pleased with at the time. As well as the heavy commuter traffic Liverpool Street provided the main line trains to East Anglia, including the boat trains to Parkeston Quay. This Thompson B1 class 4-6-0, affectionately known as 'Twelve Sixty-Four', was a regular performer on these trains. From the taxi way a father and son look down on a well-cared for locomotive, which is more than can be said for its surroundings.

MALCOLM ROOT, FGRA

Signalling Winter

Medium: Oils
Size: 61.0 x 46.0cm

When setting out to create a picture a number of points need to be established. Most importantly is the subject matter and composition, the direction of sunlight (if there is to be any) and also the mood of the picture. This brings me to 'Signalling Winter'. A very weak sun peers through the signals casting a weak shadow and highlighting the disturbed snow on the platform. The use of darker shades of blue and mauve in this part of the picture I hope destroys the illusion that snow is just white, and also creates a feeling of coldness, not welcomed by the observer on the platform. The position of the sun is such that it brings a welcome highlight to the edge of the exhaust steam and also separates the platform edge from the track as the train passes. The more unusual view of a train passing appealed to me very much, as it is something which is often seen but rarely painted.

Reference photographs play an important part in historical and technical subjects such as railways and, in this case, I was fortunate enough to have an excellent series of photographs by Geoff Silcock. Unusually, the N2 class 0-6-2T is running chimney first with its Quad-Art set of coaches through the northern London suburbs on its way to King's Cross. In those days the railways seemed to be able to operate in adverse weather conditions.

ROB ROWLAND, GRA

Night Shift

Medium: Oils
Size: 48.0 x 64.0cm

I painted this first of all as a daytime scene, but after studying photographs I had taken of the painting after it had been sold, I was struck by the notion that it would make an effective night time scene as well.

This painting is one of my favourites in terms of mood and memories. It has an air of mystery and a sense of its own time and place which I feel ought to be preserved by leaving it to the viewer to decide whether or not it is based on an actual location.

ROB ROWLAND, GRA

Waiting. Horton Road Level Crossing, Gloucester

Medium: Oils
Size: 46.0 x 36.0cm

This painting is depicted at Horton Road level crossing, Gloucester, some time in the mid to late 1950s when the Horton Road depot, Tramway Junction signalbox and the wooden gates were still in situ. Sadly, all that are left now as recognisable features in the scene are the gas holder and a building shown in the centre of the painting. The wooden gates are long gone, having been replaced by metal barrier types.

This painting, in a sense, is an observation of human behaviour, capturing the moments while waiting for a train to pass; the friendly gossip with a familiar face, the mind preoccupied with distant thoughts, and the general air of life on hold until the gates clank open, releasing those who have been waiting for the great iron wheels to rumble by.

ROB ROWLAND, GRA

The Three Pennies

Medium: Oils
Size: 56.0 x 40.0cm

Making their money grow!

ROB ROWLAND, GRA

Weekday Cross Junction

Medium: Oils
Size: 76.0 x 56.0cm

An ex-LNER Bl class 4-6-0 with a freight train heads north along the Great Central line at Nottingham, shortly before entering the tunnel which will lead out into the great cathedral-like Victoria station.

Weekday Cross holds very fond memories for me. I regularly used to catch the bus at Broad Marsh bus station and walk up and down the steps of Middle Hill by the side of the cutting wall, either into town or to and from the Lace Market in the early 1960s. I also remember an evocative night-time scene in the film *Sons and Lovers* where Paul Morel, saying goodbye to Clara, looks down the hill to the junction, and seeing the lights of the moving carriages, realises he has missed his last train home.

On a visit to Nottingham over 20 years ago, I saw a model made for a proposal to use the viaducts as a tramway system and was very saddened more recently to hear that this beautiful Great Central viaduct has now gone – demolished in 2003, only to make way for a new bridge to carry the NET (Nottingham Express Transit).

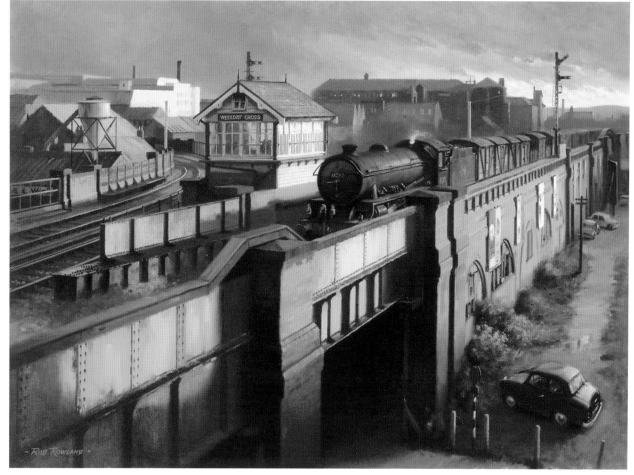

GERALD SAVINE, NDD, GRA

SBB Ae6/6 11401 Ticino on the Gotthard Lavorgno Spiral

Medium: Gouache.
Size: 59.0 x 42.0cm

The subject of the painting is Ae6/6 No. 11401 Ticino on the Lavorgno Spiral on the Gotthard route. The picture was commissioned by a member of the Swiss preservation society for the locomotive in the painting.

The Ae6/6 locomotives were giants in the motive power built for the Gotthard route over the mountains into Italy. These locomotives are being phased out of service so it was a privilege for Gerald to be asked to paint this, the first of the class. The profits from the sale of prints from the painting are to go to the preservation society.

The challenge of this painting was to depict a very well-known dramatic spiral railway scene and adapt a tall view into a composition where the viewer would not realise what had been done to compress the view. As the locomotive was not present there was also the challenge of getting the perspective and detail correct. Although the colour is strong throughout, the problem was to get a feeling of depth and three dimensions into the painting and to get the rocks and the river looking right without distracting from the subject of the painting.

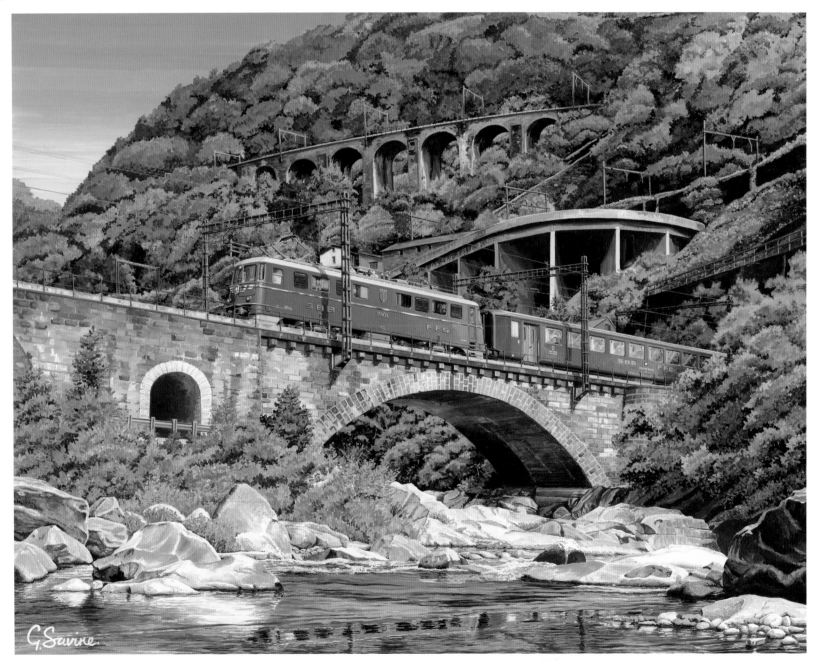

GERALD SAVINE, NDD, GRA

Autumn Colours on the Blonay–Chamby

Medium: Gouache
Size: 59.0 x 42.0cm

The subject of the painting is the metre gauge SEG (Süddeutsche Eisenbahn Gesellschaft) G 2x2 2 No. 105 locomotive crossing the dramatically sited Baye de Clarens Viaduct, with the backdrop of autumn-coloured trees. The train is preserved at the Blonay-Chamby Metre Gauge Railway Museum set in the hills above Montreux. The museum houses metre gauge steam and electric locomotives, railcars and rolling stock.

The locomotive and first coach are from the SEG in Germany, north east of Basel. The rear vehicle was a newly refurbished Bernina Railway coach.

Although Switzerland tends to be associated with electric motive power there are still many railway companies operating steam-hauled trains that can be hired and run in-between regular service trains. To be able to depict this set with the wonderful autumn colours and getting the perspective of the curved viaduct was quite challenging.

GERALD SAVINE, NDD, GRA

SBB Re6/6 11672 Balerna passing Chateau de Chillon

Medium: Gouache
Size: 59.0 x 42.0cm

The subject of the painting is the SBB Re6/6 No. 11672 *Balerna* passing the Chateau de Chillon alongside the Lac Léman (Lake Geneva) near Montreux. The train following the locomotive is of cars being transported south to Italy.

Gerald states that he loves to portray trains in their setting with plenty of small details for the viewer to look for. This typical SBB red locomotive could sum up what is thought of

as very Swiss. Many railway paintings depict passenger trains so it was a deliberate decision to produce a freight working. The train is passing the world-famous Chateau de Chillon, immortalised by Byron, with the heights of the Rochers-de-Naye rising above the clouds behind Montreux. This series of paintings depicting Switzerland brings many pleasant memories to people who view them.

G. Savine.

GERALD SAVINE, NDD GRA

MT Class 4 80104 on train to Swanage

Medium: Gouache
Size: 42.0 x 29.7cm

Gerald states that although he is not fond of painting railways as they were in the past, he does like to paint them as they are today.

The Swanage Railway today evokes childhood memories of travelling many times from London by train to Swanage in the early 1950s. So a more recent June camping holiday just outside the village of Corfe Castle, with the sound of the steam-hauled trains operating into the evenings, encouraged him to do two paintings of the line and its trains. This one shows a train leaving Corfe Castle for Swanage with the castle and Ballard Down in the background.

CRAIG TILEY, BA (HONS)

Stanier in the Snow

Medium: Acrylic
Size: 76.2 x 50.8cm (Original)

Ex-LMS 'Black 5' 4-6-0 No. 45056 storms out of Shotlock Hill Tunnel on the Settle & Carlisle line, with a fitted freight during the early 1960s. No. 45056 (originally No. 5056) was one of 842 locomotives built for the London Midland & Scottish Railway to a design by Sir William Stanier. It was from a batch of 50 built under contract by the Vulcan Foundry in 1934–35. The 'Black 5s' were regarded as one of the most successful steam locomotives ever to grace the UK rail network, and their popularity with enginemen was a result of their ability to perform on almost any duty required, whether it be a long fitted freight train, or an express passenger service.

Here, No. 45056 is depicted on the famous Settle & Carlisle railway which forged a 73-mile route across some of the most spectacular scenery in the north of England. Shotlock Hill Tunnel itself is 106 yards in length and situated just south of the line's summit at Ais Gill, between the stations of Kirby Stephen and Garsdale.

The painting is a celebration of this most successful of steam locomotive classes, shown here battling through the elements just over the summit of the long climb to Ais Gill.

CRAIG TILEY, BA (HONS)

South African Sunset

Medium: Acrylic
Size: 72.7 x 57.7cm (Original)

A South African Railways Class 25NC 4-8-4 locomotive powers up grade with a long heavy freight train in the South Africa's Free State. Some of these 3ft 6in gauge locomotives were built during the early 1950s by the North British Locomotive Company in Glasgow, and were amongst the most technically advanced and powerful steam locomotives to be built in the UK.

The massive steam locomotives employed on the SAR narrow gauge network have long held an appeal. Their sheer bulk dwarfs many UK standard gauge locomotives and they are mightily imposing to stand next to.

My aim with this painting was to capture something of the power which these locomotives exude, and to illustrate the typical duty for which they were built. Reference for the painting was fortunately made straightforward by visiting the Buckinghamshire Railway Centre to see their preserved Class 25NC, No. 3405. (*Painting reproduced courtesy of Martyn Perry.*)

MIKE TURNER, GRA

Mum, we're only going to Harrow!

Medium: Acrylic
Size: 60.0 x 45.0cm

Park Royal station on the Piccadilly Line in west London is one of Charles Holden's classic Underground station designs from the 1930s. I chose to paint this view from the westbound platform because it clearly demonstrates the uncluttered elegance of the station, from platform level to the tower, which to this day is an iconic landmark fronting the Western

Avenue. Approaching the station is a train of 1927 'Standard' stock heading for Cockfosters. The 'silver' stock came in around 1960.

Mother (wearing her NHS specs) and daughter are waiting for the Uxbridge service, taking them to South Harrow. Mother is a little distraught because she is not familiar with the tube system, but daughter is more confident!

MIKE TURNER, GRA

Royals at Willesden

Medium: Watercolour
Size: 54.0 x 36.0cm

It is 1938 and Stanier Pacific No. 6208 *Princess Helena Victoria* has just passed the locomotive depot at Willesden (the coaling tower can be glimpsed in the background), while heading north on a Liverpool express. The Acton Wells line passes over the main line at this point and the goods train crossing the bridge is a cross regional freight which originated in Feltham yard and is heading towards Cricklewood. To the right of the picture stands Acton Lane 'A' Power Station which dominated the area for many years and became a key target for bombing, along with the extensive marshalling yards during the Second World War.

I have fond memories of this location during the 1950s, a time when a youngster could cycle without fear of being run over, although on one occasion I was the target of air rifle practice by a gang of 'Rockers' outside the Ace Cafe!

On reflection, I think it was the fact that I grew up in an area dominated by railways, yards and depots that fired my enthusiasm, which in turn inspired me to paint railway scenes and foster an interest in art.

STEPHEN WARNES, BA (HONS), PGCE, GRA

Arrival

Medium: Acrylic
Size: 76.0 x 61.0cm

A spiral based on the Fibonacci number series is the prominent feature of this work. Spirals and the 'Golden Section' proportions feature in many of my paintings. The spiral is humanity's oldest symbol for spirituality – for that which is beyond us and greater than ourselves – and our emotions help connect us to it. But how can you capture in a painting the depth of emotion and the love of railways that a 14-year-old could produce? Photographic realism alone can't do it, so in this work I have called on Surrealism and Expressionist colour to help. In a year or two's time there would be parties and girls and huge new swirling whirlpools of emotion, but in 1965, railways were it for me.

The scene is my home town of Accrington's viaduct where the East Lancs line enters the station. Really, the engine should be a Stanier 'Black 5' (or 'Mickey' as I only ever knew them), but from the age of eight, a 'namer' on our line was a great treat. This one is 'Jubilee' No. 45584 *North West Frontier* which, before knowledge of the Khyber Pass into Afghanistan, always seemed appropriate for our old Victorian mill town neck of the woods.

STEPHEN WARNES, BA (HONS), PGCE, GRA

Approaching the sublime – Arnside Viaduct

Medium: Acrylic
Size: 70.0 x 60.0cm

Cumbria, my home county for over 20 years, begins with a landscape tour de force – the Kent estuary. It is one of the most beautiful in Britain and I have painted scenes of it around Sandside and Arnside for many years. After this, the line skirts the southern edge of the Lake District, brought to public awareness by the Romantic poets – and this whole area has views to stir the emotions and lift the spirit. In this scene, the London to Barrow express, hauled by a Stanier 'Black 5', moves out onto Arnside Viaduct.

The idea of the Sublime – where mankind and all its works are dwarfed by the awe-inspiring vastness and beauty of Nature is summoned up here. I particularly wanted to contrast the size of the steam locomotive – normally experienced as a huge, powerful, noisy, intimidating machine with the enormity of the sunset sky and its reflection.

ROGER WATT, GRA

'Royal Hudson' at Speed

Medium: Graphite
Size: 26.5 x 23.5cm

My desire to capture the incomparable spectacle of a steam locomotive in action was the inspiration for this drawing. Planned several weeks in advance of a rare run by Canadian Pacific 'Royal Hudson' 4-6-4 No. 2860, I scouted a location that would allow me to get the reference shots I needed . . . of the angle I wanted, and in the light that would prevail at the time of day it would be passing. The location was Crescent Beach, British Columbia, on a sunny February afternoon in 2010. Happily, my preparation paid off as I obtained a number of images from which I created the composition I had envisaged… although how the locomotive was finally framed at the 'downhill' angle, I can't say!

ROGER WATT, GRA

'Royal Hudson': Parting Shot

Medium: Graphite
Size: 15 x 12cm

'Royal Hudson': Approaching Storm

Medium: Graphite
Size: 20 x 10cm

Because of my wonderment at the unique atmosphere that only steam locomotives 'in steam' can create, I wanted to convey mood rather than record detail with these drawings of Canadian Pacific 'Royal Hudson' 4-6-4 No. 2860. My expeditions to obtain the reference photographs were necessarily carefully planned. The locations for both drawings were in British Columbia: 'Parting Shot' at Crescent Beach on a sunny February afternoon in 2010, and 'Approaching Storm' at the West Coast Railway Association Heritage Park in Squamish on a wet September day (ideal for steam effects!), in 2008.

ROGER WATT, GRA

Injector

Medium: Graphite.
Size: 25.7 x 23.0cm

I have always been intrigued by the action of light on metal surfaces, and the happy combination with my lifelong love of the steam locomotive provides a wealth of different metal textures, especially when accompanied by the attendant elements of grease, oil and corrosion. I have always preferred to draw details of locomotives as opposed to complete machines and this exhaust steam injector from an LMS tank engine (the reference for which I photographed at the National Railway Museum in 2009) exhibits all the wonderful evidence of the passage of time to make it the perfect subject for me.

DEBRA WENLOCK

No. 4 at Whitehead

Medium: Watercolour
Size: 25.5 x 37.0cm

On a visit to the Railway Preservation Society of Ireland's northern headquarters at Whitehead I came upon this magnificent view when I found the back door of the engine shed ajar. I couldn't resist painting this view of one of the society's most used engines off duty with its smokebox gleaming in the sunlight. Built immediately after Second World War and nicknamed 'Jeep', this class of loco was a useful all-rounder favoured for its reliability.

LMS NCC Class WT 2-6-4 tank loco No. 4, built in Derby in 1947, and preserved by the Railway Preservation Society of Ireland at Whitehead, County Antrim.

DEBRA WENLOCK

Downpatrick Diesel

Medium: Watercolour and gouache
Size: 25.0 x 37.0cm

In one of the furthest corners of the
Downpatrick & Co. Down Railway, I came
across this G class diesel shunter sitting disused
and forlorn at the end of a siding. I loved the
faded paintwork creating a contrast of soft
pastel colours against the strong black shadows
cast by brilliant sunshine. This simple painting
in watercolour with white gouache highlights,
lets the cream parchment paper add its own
warmth to the scene. This railway is overlooked
by Down Cathedral, beside the reputed burial
place of St Patrick.

DEBRA WENLOCK

186 at Mullingar

Medium: Acrylic
Size: 23.0 x 28.5cm

Loco No. 186 steams into Mullingar station on a
winter's afternoon. The strong sunshine filtered
through cold, damp air created a colourful
glow that couldn't be captured on camera.
The memorable atmospheric qualities of that
afternoon were a delight to recreate later in
acrylics on a warm burnt sienna background.
Mullingar was once a thriving junction station,
but only a handful of trains pass that way now.
It has been a depot for the Railway Preservation
Society of Ireland since the 1970s. No. 186 is
one of the oldest locos to still operate on the
main line in Ireland, most famously appearing
in the film *The First Great Train Robbery*
starring Sean Connery and Donald Sutherland,
masquerading as the south east of England.

ANTHONY WESTON

A Driving Ambition

Medium: Oils
Size: 50.0 x 40.0cm

The clockwork train set – surely every small boy who ever had a train set imagined himself as the driver. What could be a more exciting prospect than to be on the footplate of a mammoth steam locomotive.

JOHN E. WIGSTON, GRA

Fantasia on a Theme of Steam for R.V.W.

Medium: Watercolour
Size: 52.0 x 42.0cm

The heritage of the British Isles was well represented by railway companies that chose to name their more prestigious locomotives after historical and literal places, and persons both factual and fictional. Our musical heritage, however, was not held in the same high esteem and sadly, was neglected with only Sir Edward Elgar being acknowledged by having three locomotives named after him. Our great composers and musicians from the past 400 years, ranging from Thomas Tallis to Benjamin Britten, being either forgotten or ignored. A sad reflection on the establishment's attitude to an art the equal of our literary giants.

One War Department Austerity locomotive has been named, appropriately, *Dame Vera Lynn*, recognising the lighter side of our musical culture, but even this was after the locomotive had been privately purchased for the world of preservation. For reasons known only to the railway authorities of the period, 'Britannia' class 4-6-2 No. 70047 was alone amongst the class never being allocated a name, running its life bereft of nameplates.

In my painting I have taken the liberty of rectifying two of these omissions by naming No. 70047 after one of our great 20th century composers, Ralph Vaughan Williams. If those looking upon the painting come to the conclusion that the artist is a keen ferroequinologist, and an admirer of English music, especially that of Ralph Vaughan Williams, I can only plead guilty.

JOHN E. WIGSTON, GRA

A Gershwin Rhapsody

Medium: Watercolour
Size: 52.5 x 35.0cm

From my earliest days of railway interest I was aware of the famous Irish 800 class 4-6-0 locomotives and that they rode on a gauge of 5ft 3in, and also that several great engineers started their careers and one completed his career, at Inchicore. Beyond that my knowledge of Irish Railways was minimal until I was introduced to Julian Duroure, a tinplate O gauge enthusiast, who waxed lyrical on the railways of the 'Emerald Isles'.

His enthusiasm was catching and soon my knowledge grew when he loaned me a book *Irish Railways in Colour*. The beautiful blue livery of the Great Northern jumped from the pages; I was hooked.

Adelaide shed, Belfast, is the scene for my indulgence of the Great Northern blue. I dedicate my watercolour in memory of Julian who introduced me to the joys of Irish Railways, for which I shall always be grateful, and who unfortunately, left us at a relatively early age but is well remembered by his tinplate and Irish enthusiasts.

JOHN E. WIGSTON, GRA

It's the Royal Train

Medium: Watercolour
Size: 58.5 x 39.0cm

Right up to 1960, Fowler steam ploughing teams could be seen working the fields of East Anglia. Over the years these teams would have observed many classes of railway locomotives and different trains. This painting shows the team having completed a pull of the plough as the Royal Train, on its way to Sandringham, joins the scene.

LAWRENCE ROY WILSON, NDD, GRA, HONGRA

China's Canton–Hankow Railway

Medium: Pastel
Size: 63.0 x 47.0cm

The year was 1935; Father and I were keeping pace alongside a gigantic slow-moving 4-8-4 Chinese locomotive. No! I'm not dreaming; it is one of my most treasured childhood memories. This giant was en-route to China, on the first stage of its long journey from the Vulcan Foundry, Newton-le-Willows. Within the next eight hours or so it would have covered the 18 miles to Birkenhead Docks where it was transferred to temporary track along the quayside prior to loading aboard ship for the long sea voyage.

It was the 17th of 24 magnificent 4-8-4s built by the Vulcan Foundry for service on the Canton–Hangkow Railway. As always, this exciting operation attracted a large gathering of local people and for sure, Father and I were regulars.

At this time I would have been eight or nine years of age, and little did I know that within another seven years, following two years at technical college, I would be employed as a junior apprentice draughtsman in the drawing office at the Vulcan Foundry. Imagine my surprise and delight when many years later, semi-retired and having been appointed Honorary Public Relations Officer to the Friends of the National Railway Museum, to find one of my childhood giant locomotives returned as a gift from China, and prominently displayed within the NRM at York!

The scene I have set is of the locomotive on its home ground in China.

LAWRENCE ROY WILSON, NDD, GRA, HONGRA

First of the 'Liberation' Locomotives

Medium: Pastel
Size: 53.0 x 41.0cm

As a young apprentice in the drawing office of the Vulcan Foundry I was fortunate to witness the design and construction of many outstanding locomotives, including the 'Liberation'. Furthermore, I was to be entrusted to create during the early stages, with detailed working drawings as reference, an artist's impression of the 'Liberation' as it was to be! I was privileged to be asked to make the production drawing for the UNRRA badge which was to be fixed prominently on the cab side of each locomotive.

My enthusiasm for sketching these locomotives was rewarded by my chief, and as encouragement in my concurrent art studies, I was to receive a special pass admitting me into the silent workshops on Saturday afternoons and Sundays. Alone, I was free to sketch to my heart's content.

More than that, it gave me the opportunity to meet and to know, the very special tough, but amiable team whose responsibility it was to drive and manoeuvre the monster 'Edward Box' transporter used to ferry the really big locomotives by road to the docks at Liverpool. So it was that I managed to persuade the crew to take me along with them, seated in the rear steering control cab.

I often reflect upon my good fortune to experience such an exciting and instructive apprenticeship – thanks to my chief draughtsman.

LAWRENCE ROY WILSON, NDD, GRA, HonGRA

49 Controls – Kitson-Meyer Locomotive. Transandino, Chile

Medium: Pastel
Size: 44.5 x 57.0cm

Whilst officially retired . . . I was on my way to Chile! I had been invited to participate in the organisation of an on-going international event to be launched in Valparaiso. No connection with railways, but nevertheless, I anticipated opportunities to at least visit Santiago's Railway Museum.

What a surprise in store! Occupying prime location on the turntable was a gleaming Kitson-Meyer built in Leeds 1908, one of three designed specifically for operation on the spectacular Transandino. In conversation it was revealed that its surviving 'twin' was to be found preserved in the Los Andes Transandine depot.

It was a pleasant surprise upon arrival in Los Andes to be greeted by the staff, who were rightly proud of their depot and anxious to invite me aboard the footplate of their 'very special' locomotive, regarded universally as the most complicated, yet most successful rack/adhesion locomotives ever built. The 49 separate controls visible had been designed specifically to aid the driver negotiate the hazards expected. These included a smoke deflector lever, operating a hood to be turned over the chimney to deflect the smoke backwards throughout the numerous tunnels. Emergency braking of the 120 ton train was aided by five different built-in braking systems including 'automatic emergency', together with a swivelling headlamp facility. Truly a magnificent example of railway design and engineering.

LAWRENCE ROY WILSON, NDD, GRA, HONGRA

Transandine Depot, Los Andes, 1998

Medium: Pastel
Size: 48.5 x 36.0cm

December 1998. Arrival in Los Andes! What a magnificent view! The Transandine Depot with a backdrop of the snow-covered Andes and at the far end of the rail tracks the Kitson-Meyer, sharing its shelter from the elements with the powerful Transandino 1907 Alco Rotary Snow plough . . . all adjacent to the turntable and the busy service bays. A sure sign of the increasing tourism being enjoyed was the colourful 'Gondola' (railbus) ready to convey railway enthusiasts from around the world along the now-silent Transandine to the preserved station at Rio Blanco.

Together with Victor Hugo (good friend and interpreter), we were to meet during my return to Santiago with the most senior railway official, Jaime Contreras, Gerente de Normalizacion y Control. We were graciously conducted to the board room to a very warm and friendly reception, and a highly detailed resume of the government's recently launched 'Railway Heritage – Preservation Project'. Then came the big surprise, our host would like to invite me as his 'Guest of Honour' to participate in the inaugural run of a Temuco–Valdivia steam service scheduled within the next few days. The big surprise of the day was the on-board interview by a Valdivia TV camera team and a journalist for Chile's premier newspaper *El Mercado* (an article reproduced at length appeared in the following day's issue).

The warm hospitality and personal attention experienced including the surprise footplate adventure will remain for ever as the highlight of my Chile tours.

LAWRENCE ROY WILSON, NDD, GRA, HONGRA

Konya Sheds, Turkey

Medium: Pastel
Size: 63.0 x 48.0cm

In 1939, a contract was placed in this country by the Turkish State Railways (TCDD) for a number of Class 1E freight locomotives of a previous German design, but due to the intervention of the war, the order was not completed until 1948. Twenty-two of these engines were built at the Vulcan Foundry, Newton-le-Willows, for operation on the difficult and mountainous main lines in Asia Minor, radiating from Ankara and Eskisehir.

BIOGRAPHIES OF THE ARTISTS

Peter Annable, GRA

After leaving art college, Peter Annable was offered an apprenticeship in a design studio and was employed as a commercial artist/designer. As a young artist working in this environment he was subject to many influences and at that time of life, found it a stimulating and instructive experience. He states that he learned so much from the late Robert Forrester, an excellent watercolourist, who stressed to him the importance of the need to sketch and draw for at least thirty minutes every day, and to take trips into the countryside to paint from life. Robert would tell Peter that 'The important thing in art is Emotion, you have got to be moved by something before you can ever paint it.'

In 1997, Peter decided to venture out on his own, producing designs for the packaging industry and decorated containers and tins, for which he received many design awards, book and brochure illustrations, and teaching watercolour painting. Currently, Peter is working part time within the offender learning sector teaching all aspects of art and design. He is a member of both Nottingham and Mansfield societies of artists and enjoys painting a wide variety of subjects including landscapes and portraits, selling his work throughout the UK and abroad.

Peter states that whatever painting he is working on, from atmospheric impressionistic landscapes in oils, to delicate watercolour paintings, he tries to retain his own personality in the subject.

Chris Ashmore, GRA

Chris Ashmore was born in 1952 in the Metropolitan Borough of Whitechapel in the east end of London. He grew up to his late teens living in Stepney and Canning Town. Chris obtained a passion for steam trains having seen their demise in the late 1960s. Always remembering the 'Golden Arrow', as it steamed by the farm where he stayed with his dear Nan and Grandad, who used to take him hop-picking with them in the late 1950s and early 1960, Chris states 'Wow, what a great time I had down on the hop farms around Goudhurst and Paddock Wood in Kent. Watching trains go by. Raiding the orchard now and then with the other children, whose mums and dads were in the hop fields. Life was so uncomplicated then . . . I sometimes wish I could turn the clock back.'

He left London in the early 1970s and moved to Thetford, in Norfolk where he has been living to date with his partner Jen. He tends to specialise in transportation subjects, mainly railroad locomotives and heavy road vehicles. Chris's principle interests are heavy electric locomotives, articulated locomotives, and American interurban locomotives. He is currently the coordinator for the South East and East Anglia Group of the Guild of Railway Artists.

John Austin FGRA

In 1987, John Austin moved to an old three-storey house on the banks of the River Severn in Bridgnorth, Shropshire, close to the northern terminus of the Severn Valley Railway. This was in order to realise his childhood ambition of becoming a full-time artist specialising in railways. His work has become synonymous with the SVR having painted their annual timetable leaflet picture for 22 years.

In 1992, John joined the Guild of Railway Artists and has tried to exhibit at every exhibition of the Guild. He has been successful in winning the 'Picture of the Year Award' on 17 occasions. He was made an Honorary Fellow of the Guild in 2006 and is currently the Guild's Deputy President.

John's work consists mainly of commissions which provide him with the opportunity to travel to various locations and preserved railways for research. He now spends time in both Shropshire and Devon. The famous stretch of railway in south Devon between Starcross and Teignmouth has provided the inspiration for many of his stormy sea paintings and is the perfect place to portray the drama of steam locomotives. A book of his work, entitled *Smoke, Steam & Light* has recently been published by Haynes.

Eric Bottomley, GRA

Eric was born in Oldham, Lancashire in 1948. Growing up in the environs of the industrial North he and his young contemporaries spent their spare time around the railways and canals of that area. Little did he know that these images would, in adulthood, manifest themselves on canvas. Eric studied for three years at Oldham School of Art, leaving in 1964 to enter the world of advertising, in Manchester.

In 1974, he moved to Dorset, continuing as a freelance artist/illustrator which enabled him to devote more time to oil painting. He took up painting full time in 1976, from his studio in Wimborne Minster. Gaining Equity membership in 1972 through his work in theatre, Eric supplemented his income in the early years by doing walk-on/extra work for TV and films. This proved very useful for his period costume Victorian and Edwardian paintings, working from his own photographs.

He joined the Guild of Railway artists in 1979, later to become a Full Member. In 1988, Eric and his wife Jeanette moved to the village of Much Marcle in Herefordshire where, along with carrying out much commissioned work, he now teaches art and publishes his wide range of fine art prints and cards

A professional artist in oils and gouache for more than 35 years, Eric has had a book of his work published.

Gerald Broom, GRA

Perhaps I am a storyteller, as like the first cave dwellers, I need to express what I see. When I left school in 1960 I hadn't a clue about life or what to do next, but I did have some sort of awareness of things around me. So I taught myself music and how to paint, both suspect and a struggle ever since!

I am sure everyone will recognise the influences of my work, but emotions, railways, art, how long have you got? Nostalgia has now become so fashionable that it gives a new definition to vicarious. But railways are an engineering subject, the realistic and practical side of historical development, and in the arts the subject was already neglected in a railway 'golden age' when society was uneasy with such a vulgar genre, and very few images from what I would suggest is a pre-camera emotion. So I presumptuously set out to try to depict that gap, to try and re-create images from the past, inspired by the unquestionable masterful techniques of the English Schools.

Involvement and commitment to the subject would have to echo Stubbs and Rembrandt in the dissection of cadavers, so I did that with a hands-on experience of all things railway preservation, but on reflection, perhaps that in itself can dilute the mystique of an emotion? However, I think railway art will still be a valid personal product of observation, but then I am an historian.

Jonathan Clay

I was born in Blackburn in 1950, and still live there, although I have made several attempts to escape. I come from an artistic background.

My father was an art teacher and a well-known artist locally. His father and elder brother were also very talented and I still possess examples of all their works. I don't recall ever being given any formal instruction by Dad but something has rubbed off along the way. Some say it's generic, since my youngest daughter is also an art teacher!

My introduction to railways was at a very early age, and although Dad was no trainspotter he could tell the difference between a V2 and an A3 at a distance. My childhood was spent train and bus spotting. Holidays were spent in North Wales and I discovered narrow gauge preservation in its formative years.

I had no thoughts of a career in art and was steered towards the sciences at school. I married young and acquired a family in fairly short order, so had little opportunity to pursue my artistic aims. I did have sporadic attempts during the 1970s and '80s, but was always overcome by the need to earn a living.

By 1998, my children had fled the nest and I was totally dissatisfied with working for someone else. This led me to think seriously about making a career in art. With developments in computers and reprographics it meant that it was now affordable. Although it was a gamble it has paid off.

Over the past twelve years I have painted nearly 1,000 pictures – not all of them railway subjects. More importantly, however, I have travelled extensively and discovered that the railway movement contains some of the nicest people in the world, many of whom I now count as friends.

Now that I have achieved the age of the bus-pass I am not sure how much longer I will carry on – but I have no intention of retiring just yet!

Matthew Cousins, GRA

Matthew Cousins was born in 1953 at Hitchin, next to the East Coast Main Line. His childhood memory of railways was the summer Sunday afternoon walk down to Cadwell crossing to watch the Gresley A4 streamliners flashing past at high speed. Railways have always fired his

imagination and whilst he still has memories of steam trains, he regrets not being able to see the trains in the 1930s when they were at the high-point of steam locomotion. The posters that he has created for this book are from that era and portray the best locomotives of Sir Nigel Gresley, the A4s and P2s.

He welcomed the formation of the Guild of Railway Artists which he joined in 1980, having also joined the Bluebell Railway as a working volunteer two years earlier. The Guild he says, has enabled him to meet and learn from other like-minded artists and to make some lasting friendships. Matthew worked for ten years on the locomotive footplate, which has given him a real appreciation of the life of an engineman. He has always loved the old railway posters and decided to develop a poster-art style of painting. From 1996 Matthew has supplied the artwork for the Bluebell Railway's annual timetable leaflets.

The preservation of old railways has been a real motivation for him and he took the opportunity in 1998 to restore a large railway luggage van (formerly used in the 'Golden Arrow' Pullman train), based at Horsted Keynes on the Bluebell Railway. He has since fully refurbished it with the help of other volunteers and has put it to use as a railway art exhibition coach for use by rail artists in the South East.

John Cowley, GRA

John Cowley is Bedfordshire born and this is where he began a 25-year career in car body design. Although he has never pursued any formal art training he has benefited from those years spent in model-making, draughtsmanship and illustration; the technical appreciation aids him in constructing railway paintings. He will tell you that patience developed through his work was probably the most significant legacy that he acquired.

He works in both oils and watercolour and has recently taken to first producing a basic watercolour ground on Indian rag paper, and then after mounting to board and sealing, he finalises the painting in oils before varnishing with hard MSA. This enables the painting to be framed without glass. Another recent process involves calico mounted to board and painting in oils; sanding back and completing with many glazes helps to achieve that hint of impressionism.

His abiding love and memories of the gritty sheds and yards still inspires him most, but he doesn't want to diminish his other interest, which is the landscape. A recent move to Cornwall has re-charged his desire to wander around the Helford creeks and search out those wistful scenes.

John is grateful that in 1997, the Guild of Railway Artists elected him as Full Member and he continues to produce commissions as well as exhibit when possible.

Frederick C.B. Cox

As far back as I can remember, I have always been interested in art. At infants school I was presented with a little book titled *How to Draw Ships*, which I still have today.

All through my school days, I was involved with many art projects. On leaving main school I went on to art college, but being totally disillusioned with the course I was on, left the college after six months and started work in the real world, thereby helping my parents in the process. Later, marriage, family and mortgage meant that work was top priority, while art was put on the back burner for a time.

My introduction to painting the railway scene was brought about by a friend, who asked me to paint a picture of the 'Flying Scotsman' leaving King's Cross. The bug had bitten hard, for I started studying railway books and learning as much as possible about all aspects of railway – a fascinating subject to behold.

After researching for a commission, I strive to create a high level of detail in my paintings. The overall subject is given my full attention. Having completed many drawings and paintings since that first time, the next one will command the same enthusiasm. Art is a wonderful gift to possess and I feel honoured to be a very small part of the art world.

Ian Docwra

Ian Docwra has had a passion for railways since he was a child, and his father took him to see his first Southern steam-hauled trains in the 1960s. He was born in 1961, brought up in Surrey and still lives in Epsom, with his wife and dog.

His father was also a railway enthusiast and worked as a signal engineer for London Underground for 40 years. He was part of the team that introduced automatic train operation to the Victoria line in 1967.

Ian is a keen railway photographer and his photographs are often published in *The Railway Magazine* and *Steam Railway* magazine. The A1 Steam Trust has recently requested to use his photographs for their publicity. He started painting (in water colours) in his late teens but then moved to oils soon after. He has had a couple of exhibitions of his work and has completed many commissioned pieces on transport and architectural subjects. He also enjoys landscape painting. Ian is currently a business analyst with Transport for London.

Michael Flanders

Michael Flanders was born in Bristol in 1963, where he lives today with his family. He did not follow the usual route of further education and art training. Using his artistic talents he was employed directly from school by his father, Barrie Flanders, as an airbrush artist, until branching out into graphics as a freelance graphic designer. This was his career for a number of years, and following this, Michael has had several career changes before finally taking his raw, self-taught, artistic talents seriously a few years ago and lifting the brushes on a more regular basis. His ultimate ambition is to pursue painting full-time in the future.

Michael has a varied range of work and enjoys painting many subjects, including landscapes and anything mechanical. Amongst these, the biggest challenge is creating the atmosphere and drama required by his railway art.

In 2009, he made contact with the Guild of Railway Artists and was duly assessed to be of a standard acceptable to join the Guild as an

Associate Member. Having entered work in the Guild's Railart 2009 exhibition he was elated to find his painting 'On the Turntable' voted for by the public, in second place in the 'Picture of the Year' competition. A great achievement and his next aim is to produce work worthy to become a Full Member of the Guild.

Ray Gale

Ray's career began in education and later progressed to being a part-time, self-employed artist, developing an interest in printmaking, specialising in producing original screen prints.

His main interest is in the structure and pattern of industrial scenes depicting machines, for example, the construction of motorways and railways, or people at work in the factory or brewery. Industrial commissions have been undertaken for national companies using the technique of screen printing – utilising a combination of line drawing and colour print.

Mike Gunnell GRA, AGAvA

Specialisation: watercolours and chromacolour – railways, aviation, landscapes and ecclesiastical buildings. Born in Hull in 1937, Mike moved with his family to Withernsea on the Holderness coast, a few months before the outbreak of the Second World War. His interest in railways developed at an early age, on the knee of his maternal grandfather, a retired LNER signalman. His paternal grandfather was also a signalman and two great grandfathers were railway guards.

Mike followed a science course through school and university followed by three years in the RAF as a ground radar fitter. He joined Blackburn Aircraft where he worked on the Buccaneer strike bomber when a change of career took him into primary school teaching. He retired after twenty years, in 1991, and began to teach painting and drawing for leisure-learning classes in Humberside. This continued in Ipswich after remarrying in 2001.

He joined the railway and aviation artists' guilds in 1994 and is now a Full Member of the former and an associate of the latter. He exhibits regularly at the guilds' exhibitions and is currently the organiser of events held in the East Anglian region of the GAvA.

Nick Hardcastle, MA (RCA), GRA

I studied illustration at Maidstone College of Art and the Royal College of Art, graduating with an MA in 1981. For most of my career I worked as a freelance illustrator in London, although I am now based in the Totnes area in Devon.

My career has stretched across a very wide area from publishing to advertising, design, architectural and editorial work. My clients include the London-based broadsheets, many well-known magazines and publishers, as well as a wide variety of corporate clients. I mainly work with pen and ink and watercolour, and I thrive on challenging or obscure briefs!

I have a passion for paintings and photographs that capture a particular atmosphere or effects of light, and photo-realistic painting. Creating photo-realistic artwork is incredibly time-consuming for me, but does I feel, showcase my particular skills.

Some notable commissions from my clients have included a series of illustrated panels on the walls of Wapping Underground station, a drawing of the Royal Train for InterCity that was presented to the Queen and which resides in the library at Windsor Castle, and a poster for London Underground called 'Or take the Tube', which won an award sponsored by Elfande for the best conceptual illustration.

John Hardy, GRA

John was born in north east London and his love of railways stems from journeys in wartime and later on the Great Western in the 1940s. As childhood progressed clear memories of many railway scenes remain, as do his early attempts to draw them. The attitudes of people around him varied but nevertheless he was inspired by great artists and designers who created rail subjects in every media.

An art-bias course at technical school was followed by a career in the marketing sector of the advertising industry, covering many aspects of graphic design, left little time to paint. The railway enthusiasm never dimmed however and on becoming freelance latterly he took on more illustration work.

Truly inspirational was an exhibition seen in London showing works and promoting an earlier Guild of Railway Artists' book in the early 1990s. This urged him to join these like-minded people and make up for lost time.

John Harrison, ATD, GRA

One of the few advantages of advancing years is that one can recall vivid impressions of many past decades. I still retain clear mental images of the 1950s when I was at art college, followed by National Service in the Army Education Corps, and then my first appointment as a secondary school art teacher. I can also picture the 1940s when I attended grammar school, surprisingly unaffected by the war. I even have memories of the 1930s – a small boy travelling with my parents on the LMS to Blackpool, Southport, Liverpool and even on parts of the West Coast Main Line. Red 'Jubilees', red 'Scots', red carriages – even the Mersey electric trains were red in those days.

I suppose the period most deeply etched on my memory is the late 1950s and '60s when I taught in a secondary modern school and then became Head of Art in a large comprehensive. In those days I came into almost daily contact with the recently nationalised railways before we had heard of Dr Beeching. Smoke and steam were then a part of daily life – from the railways and from the many local industries. Indeed, nearly all our homes burned coal in those days.

How the scene (and the atmosphere) has changed since then! It is hardly surprising that many of my paintings reflect these changes as I try to recapture the vanished scenes of my youth. I would only add that I have no longing to return to the smoke and grime of the past, and I certainly do not mourn the passing of the age of steam.

Philip D. Hawkins, FGRA

Philip D. Hawkins has been considered for many years to be one of Britain's foremost railway artists. His paintings have been reproduced in many forms, including fine-art prints, calendars, greeting cards and collectors' plates, as well as appearing regularly in magazines and books. Much of his output is to commission for commercial concerns, particularly the railway industry (Virgin Trains, DB Schenker, Docklands Light Railway, and Eurostar being among his many clients), and private individuals.

He was a founder member of the Guild of Railway Artists and the Guild's President from 1988 until 1998, when he was made a Fellow of the Guild, at that time only the third artist to be so honoured (following David Shepherd and the late Terence Cuneo). Two superb books based on his work have been published: *Tracks on Canvas* in 1998 (reprinted in 2001, 2005, 2006 and 2009) and *Steam On Canvas*, in 2005. Born and brought up in the West Midlands, he attended the Birmingham College of Art and Design. He now lives and works in Devon.

His evocative paintings not only capture the atmosphere of the railway but also represent its very essence. This ability to both appreciate the unique atmosphere and understand its workings emanates from a life-long love of steam locomotives and of railways in general, an interest developed during the artist's formative years in the West Midlands during the 1950s.

Chris Holland, GRA

Chris was born in Wigan in 1946 and currently resides in the town. He had an ability to paint from a very early age and became interested in railways during the 1950s, The natural results were many paintings of steam locomotives being produced while he was at school. After leaving school the painting ceased until 1976, when more work was produced, culminating in sales and exhibitions. He is completely self-taught and has worked mainly in oils, acrylics and gouache. The most notable dates for Chris were in 1979 and 1983 when he had works accepted for the Royal Academy Summer Exhibition in London. He appeared on Granada TV's 'Granada Reports' and also on the BBC TV 'Newsnight' as a result of the RA exhibitions. During this period he also exhibited at the Manchester Academy.

During the 1990s, Chris produced some Lake District landscapes (as well as his locomotives) in a photo-realistic style which he has now perfected. Working mainly in gouache or acrylics, his paintings display a depth and integrity rarely found in watercolours. His fine draughtsmanship skills, attention to detail and ability to capture the lifelike realism of the subject combine to make his work much sought after. Examples are in a growing number of collections.

In 2000, Chris became an Associate Member of the Guild of Railway Artists, and has exhibited work at most 'Railart' exhibitions since that time. He was elected to Full Membership in 2004.

John Hughes, GRA

I was told my introduction to railways was in a push-chair at Snow Hill station, which is right and proper for a 'Brummie', sadly I don't recall the incident. Later, aged 11/12 I was taken to view the wonders of Smallheath & Sparkbrook station at which I spent a good deal of the next few years, studiously noting the numbers of passing engines, obviously of great educational benefit. The station was a very busy place, with goods yards on either side of the line to the north, and Tyseley engine shed to the south. It also fostered a lifelong passion for railways.

I started painting in 1983 but two to three years passed before logic suggested the two passions could be combined. I joined the Guild in 1983 and some of my output has been railway ever since. Can I emphasise the word 'railways'. I try not to paint trains, my interest is in the ambience of the railway scene. With regard to the theme of this book, I don't suppose any artist would tackle a picture unless there was an emotional content, whether this is perceived by an audience is another matter.

Bernard Jones, NDD, ATC, GRA

Born in Horley, Surrey, in 1943, Bernard Jones commenced his art training in 1960 at Reigate School of Art, obtaining an NDD in painting and printmaking. He completed his studies at Brighton College of Art with an art teacher's certificate. From 1966 to 1971, he took a full-time teaching post at St Wilfred's RC Comprehensive School in Crawley and became Head of the Art Department in 1968. In 1971, he took leave of teaching to produce hand-thrown stoneware pottery full-time at Holmbury St Mary in Surrey. He moved to Beaford, Devon, in 1974 and set up Beaford Pottery – he also built a large OO gauge layout.

In 1986, Bernard began full-time railway painting, moving to Hatherleigh, Devon, in 1988. He also began at this time, his regular shows of his work at Bridgnorth station on the Severn Valley Railway during the Spring and Autumn Gala weekends.

Bernard now resides with his family at Splatt, Broadwood Kelly, Devon. He continues painting in oils, exhibiting his work in the buffet at Okehampton station, working to commissions, and exhibiting with the Guild.

Wynne B. Jones, GRA

Born at Rossett, near Wrexham in 1950, Wynne B. Jones's first notable artistic success came in the early 1960s when he was chosen to exhibit at the Royal Cambrian Academy, Conway, in a children's exhibition. Following a long career in the oil industry, during which the opportunity to paint was limited, he took early retirement at the end of 1996 to concentrate on his art.

Wynne joined the Guild in 1999 and has been privileged to serve on the Guild Council both as an associate and Full Member. As a member of the Guild, he has exhibited regularly at various venues including the National Railway Museum at York, its outstation Locomotion at Shildon, Kidderminster Railway Museum, and at Steam in Swindon, as well as various galleries throughout the United Kingdom.

Wynne is a member of the Wirral Society of Arts and exhibits regularly at the Williamson Art

Gallery and Museum, Birkenhead. His work has been published as greetings cards by various leading UK publishers and his paintings are held in private, public and corporate collections throughout the UK, Ireland and the USA.

Morgan Lewis

Morgan's creative instincts began to emerge at school where he displayed an aptitude for art and technical drawing. He dabbled with railway pictures in these early years but it is only in the last ten years that his interest has become more intensive.

All his current work is in oils. Some more recent pictures have evolved into an alternative style inspired by the great railway poster artists. Morgan's other interests include walking, cooking and sports cars.

Kevin Parrish

Birmingham born in 1953, Kevin has been interested in steam locomotives from his childhood. One Christmas around 1960, he received *The Observer's Book of Steam Locomotives of Britain* (1958 edition) as a present. He used to study this book avidly, learning about the specifications and types of locomotives therein. The book became rather tatty with pages falling out through constant referral, however, he has more recently found a second-hand copy which has been kept well preserved.

He became particularly interested in the Pacific-type locomotives from the LNER and LMS and used to pencil sketch them from his mind's eye in his spare time. They looked majestic and powerful to him and he could see that they were a wonderful piece of British engineering.

The railway is just one of his subject areas. Other genre include various forms of transport, landscape and portraiture. His work has been shown on exhibition at a number of galleries mostly within the Midlands and has been reproduced in a number of forms of merchandise such as greetings cards, jigsaw puzzles, calendars, CD covers etc.

Kevin is a traditional freehand oil painter and has been painting full time since 1995. He began working in colour but now also uses a black and white (monochrome) style. He paints from dark to light, with highlights sometimes consisting of several layers of paint.

Brian Robinson

My interest in painting began in my early childhood and has continued without interruption most of my life. After art school, I pursued a career in graphic design for more than 45 years which latterly included running a training business teaching computer graphics.

I like to experiment with various techniques and media including acrylics, pastels, collage and mixed media, but my main interest remains watercolour, usually on gesso. Although I like to paint many different subjects my main focus is on the steam railway period where I attempt to depict the more prosaic side of the era, trying to conjure up the smoke and grime of the ordinary working environment whilst at the same time seeking to capture the poignancy of neglect and dereliction. I work from my own photographs of locomotives and rolling stock etc. combined with information gleaned from old photographs for details of buildings and the industrial landscape.

Along with my wife Maggie I tutor local art groups and run art breaks and holidays in the UK, France and Portugal. My work has been exhibited and sold all the over the country and for the past few years my train paintings have been in the Royal Institute of Painters in Watercolour annual exhibition in the Mall Galleries.

Malcolm Root, FGRA

Malcolm Root was born in 1950, just in time to enjoy the last years of steam on Britain's railways. Having been born and bred in North Essex he was always going to have a soft spot for the Great Eastern Railway and especially the old Colne Valley Railway, which ran through his home town of Halstead.

On leaving school he joined the printing trade with a view to a career in typography, but left in 1981 to become a professional artist. Football has always been an important hobby of Malcolm's. As a child he played in the fields adjoining the railway line and as a young man he played for local clubs. Now he contents himself on a Saturday afternoon watching Colchester United from the stands. Inspiration also comes from real ale and he has long been a member of CAMRA (Campaign for Real Ale). Malcolm is married to Meryl and they have two grown-up daughters Georgina and Josephine.

Four books of Malcolm's paintings have been published and reproductions of his work can also be seen on calendars, greetings cards, collectors' plates and jigsaw puzzles. Original paintings hang in many collections, both private and public. Malcolm Root was elected as an Honorary Fellow of the Guild in 2010 – the highest accolade the Guild pays to a member artist.

Rob Rowland, GRA

Rob Rowland was born and brought up in the Midlands in the 1950s and '60s and throughout his time at school his one ambition was to work in the professional art industry. He began work in a picture restoration studio and went on to graduate from Gloucestershire College of Arts and Technology.

It was during his employment in the art and design department of a national brewery, while working on themes to coincide with the GWR 150th anniversary celebrations in 1985, that he became fascinated with depicting railways in his own paintings. This later developed into an interest in other aspects of our industrial heritage.

Rob became a member of the Guild of Railway Artists in 1987 and was elected a Full Member in 1999. He has been painting professionally since 1990.

Gerald Savine, NDD, GRA

Born in London in October 1945, Gerald Savine attended the Harrow School of Art from 1959 until 1965, including three years studying fine-art and a three-year NDD course in commercial design. His thesis for the NDD was, perhaps prophetically, 'Railway Liveries – 1923–1948'.

Originally, he worked in advertising agencies in London, before moving to Bristol and heading up a creative department. Eventually moving to an agency in Cheltenham, he went independent in 1979, working in all areas of advertising, graphic design, exhibition design and illustration for local, national and international clients. Around 1990, he started painting marine subjects and had a number of commissions from the UK and Europe.

Through an interest in modelling Swiss railways, and being a member of the Swiss Railway Society, he started painting Swiss railway and lake paddle boat subjects, producing limited-edition prints which are collected worldwide. As well as exhibiting around the UK his paintings have been exhibited at the Verkehrshaus, the Swiss National Transport Museum in Lüzern. Gerald's work has also appeared in publications in the USA, China and Japan. He has produced paintings of British railway subjects including a commission for a number of locomotive profile paintings for the *British Steam Railways* part work.

Nine years ago he started art classes/ workshops and painting holidays for amateur artists, and currently runs a number of classes each week with people coming from around the South and West Midlands. Gerald works primarily in gouache and only occasionally in oils or watercolour.

Craig Tiley, BA (Hons)

Born in Swindon in 1983, and although only a stone's throw from the home of the GWR, Craig Tiley arrived too late to appreciate first-hand the famous railway works, and only has a few memories of 'A-Shop', as a pile of rubble. Inspired by Terence Cuneo, he has been painting and drawing as long as he can remember, and his interest in art continued throughout his education. This culminated in 2005 with the gaining of a BA (Hons) in design. Preferred mediums are pencils and acrylics, and he receives regular commissions – his first gained when he was only 14 years old. His work now resides in private collections throughout the UK, Europe and the USA.

In 2001, Craig won First Great Western's competition to design a poster for the launch of the 'Adelante' passenger trains, his winning poster being displayed at all stations between Bristol and Paddington.

The Railway Magazine, Steam World, Heritage Railway and *Wingspan*, are just some of the publications to include Craig's artwork, and in 2004 the Isle of Man Post Office featured one of his paintings on a stamp to celebrate the bi-centennial anniversary of steam. In 2006, a portrait was selected for the BP Portrait Award at the National Portrait Gallery, London. His painting of Bulleid's controversial 'Leader' locomotive was used as the cover illustration for a book by Kevin Robertson in 2007. As well as gaining membership of the GRA, he is also a member of the Guild of Aviation Artists and the Guild of Motoring Artists.

Mike Turner, GRA

I spent my early years in north-west London where the railway environment proved to be of great interest to me. I went on to study graphic design at High Wycombe College, gaining a diploma in art and design. Further studies at the London College of Printing enabled me to gain a City and Guilds in technical graphics. I worked as a layout artist/illustrator for the publishing industry including a four-year stint at the *Sunday Times*.

Since the early 1980s, I have worked professionally as a freelance illustrator specialising, mainly but not exclusively, in railway subjects, depicting scenes from home and abroad, ancient and modern. My work has been published in numerous magazines, newspapers and books. I have exhibited work within the United Kingdom and I have pictures in collections in New York, Germany, France and Switzerland, as well as in the UK.

My interest in art takes me on visits to many art galleries and exhibitions. I enjoy painting and drawing portraits, landscapes and other figurative work as well as railway subjects.

Stephen Warnes, BA (Hons), PGCE, GRA

Stephen Warnes was born in north-east Lancashire and graduated from Essex University with a degree in the Theory and History of Art. He has been a Full Member of the Guild of Railway Artists since 1994.

He received his first public commission, 'A Painting to Celebrate the Centenary of the Glasgow Underground' in 1997, and in the same year had works exhibited at Tullie House Museum in Carlisle alongside paintings by Terence Cuneo and photographs by Eric Treacy, at the exhibition for the 150th anniversary of Carlisle Citadel station. He had a retrospective exhibition in 1999, and in 2006 returned to his native area with a very well-received exhibition in Blackburn Museum and Art Gallery entitled 'Deep Roots'. In that year also, his painting 'Smile Boys - That's the Style (the Accrington Pals)' was shown at the Haworth Art Gallery, Accrington, with paintings loaned from the Imperial War Museum by Paul Nash and C.R.W. Nevinson in an exhibition commemorating the 90th anniversary of the Battle of the Somme. In 2010 he completed a commission for the Ravenglass & Eskdale Railway Preservation Society to mark their Golden Jubilee.

He has lived for more than 20 years in Cumbria and as well as railway subjects, he is known for painting light-filled Cumbrian landscapes.

Roger Watt, GRA

Growing up in the post-war years north of London, my older brother and I would frequently pack our lunches and head off for a day of trainspotting with our dad who, being a professional artist himself, passed on his passion to me, for both for steam locomotives and drawing. This developed into a fascination for exploring the inherent complexity of light reacting with metal surfaces using just the most basic of materials . . . pencil and paper.

At 18, I entered Watford School of Art where my drawing tutor, Tony Millard, became my second major influence through instilling in me the importance of drawing what I see, and not putting any mark down on paper 'unless it is right'.

After leaving art school, I embarked on a career as art director in the field of international magazine publishing; this led to me being headhunted by one of Europe's largest and most innovative art publishing companies as publishing director. My drawings have been shown at the Royal Academy Summer Exhibition and, with the GRA, at the National Railway Museum in York. Currently, I exhibit, lecture on drawing and the creative industry, and am an art consultant with a leading international publisher of fine-art prints based in San Francisco.

I live in Vancouver, where my greatest influences today come from my daughter Robyn and my son Laurence, who continuously challenge me to become a better person. I am represented by Folio of London

Debra Wenlock

Debra Wenlock grew up in Rugby, Warwickshire – the important railway junction town and home of rugby football. One of her earliest memories is of her great grandmother's steam-powered arrival at the Great Central Railway station and two of her uncle's worked as firemen before the electric trains took over. At the age of four, she remembers going with her father to collect a large second-hand train set – they are still fighting over its ownership!

Gaining a degree in textile design at Loughborough College of Art in 1987, Debra enjoyed the variety of design as well as painting and drawing for their own sake.

She has been employed as a designer and an illustrator, and has more than a decade's experience as a freelance designer of such products as furnishing fabrics, wall-coverings, and more recently, railway posters and museum display panels.

Debra moved to Northern Ireland in 1993 and was amazed by the tremendous enthusiasm and nostalgia for old transport of one vintage or another. Since then, barely a day has gone by without these subjects figuring largely and it was almost inevitable that they should come to dominate her work. Debra lives in Groomsport, Co. Down and enjoys depicting her adopted home, its surroundings and its history in her work. Her book and exhibition of paintings of the legendary Ards Tourist Trophy races were both sell out successes.

Anthony Weston

Anthony Weston was born in Hednesford, Staffordshire, in 1944. He is a self-taught artist working in oils. Education included a course at Tottenham Polytechnic School of Building. Qualifications are a GCE in painting and decorating. For the past fifty years he has worked as a professional signwriter. He currently resides in Calvados, France.

John E. Wigston, GRA

John E. Wigston was born at Redhill, Surrey, in 1939, but spent most of his early life in Chingford, Essex. After initial training in horticulture, three years in the RAF and two years with llford Films at Brentwood, he joined ICI on Teesside and remained with the company for 27 years.

All his life, transport has fascinated him, especially railways. It was natural therefore for transport to be the earliest subject for his other hobby, painting. His art began to take on more importance when he attended evening classes at Hartlepool College of Art. Receiving encouragement from his family, the college and colleagues at lCl, he had his first one-man

exhibition at the Gray Art Gallery, Hartlepool in 1970.

Several exhibitions followed, including the Museum of British Transport, Clapham, together with commissions, most notably the celebrations for the 150th anniversary of the Stockton & Darlington Railway.

Being involved with HMS *Warrior*, when being restored at Hartlepool, his marine painting took on more importance, having already completed several painting of Royal Navy ships. One had been purchased by the officers of HMS *Hermes* and another by the Fleet Air Arm Museum.

John is also very much involved with traction engines, the A1 Locomotive Trust, and is a member of the Swedish Railway Society – steam keeps him busy. He has also been an Artist in Residence on the 'QE2', for several premier cruises, and at the National Railway Museum. One of his most recent commissions was for the Svitzer Towing Company for a painting of the QE2 on its last departure from Southampton.

Lawrence Roy Wilson, NDD, GRA, HonGRA

Born in Wolverton, Buckinghamshire in 1926, Lawrence Roy Wilson's career commenced at the Vulcan Foundry Ltd as an apprentice draughtsman. This included accompanying the company photographer, recording the transshipment of Vulcan locomotives to railways around the world. Technical and art education included evening art school tuition at St Helens Gamble Institute followed by a scholarship to Manchester School of Art, and graduation with a National Diploma in design. His career progressed into working as a studio artist for a Manchester advertising agency, leading to appointment as a publicity manager in the aeronautical industry.

A new career in promotion design and organisation of international trade fairs around the world culminated in a two-month project in Moscow in 1961. Extensive world travel then commenced for over four decades, involving visits to no fewer than 70 countries. Throughout

these travels every opportunity was taken to pursue a life-long love for railways and a return to painting.

Semi-retirement presented an opportunity to stage by invitation, a three-month solo exhibition of his work in 2002 at the National Railway Museum, with more than 40 paintings and sketches on display. Two works were retained by the museum for their archives. Voluntary relationship with the Museum continued as Artist in Residence and as Honorary Public Relations Officer to the Friends of the NRM.

Roy gained Associate Membership of the Guild in 1996 and Full Membership in 1999. In 2001, he was honoured with Honorary Membership for services to the Guild of Railway Artists and in 2005 elected as President of the Guild, a position he still holds with great pleasure.

INDEX OF ARTISTS